umai

umai

Recipes From a Japanese Home Kitchen

Millie Tsukagoshi Lagares

Photography by Lizzie Mayson and Lucy Laucht

For my mum and dad.

For keeping me fed,
inspired and smiling
at all times.

8	introduction
12	about this book
14	a note on Japanese flavours
16	the Japanese pantry
26	kitchen tools
28	the heart of Japanese home cooking
32	easy lunches
78	family favourites
134	izakaya at home
198	desserts
222	where to buy Japanese ingredients
224	menu suggestions
226	index
236	acknowledgements
238	about the author

introduction はじめに

The first thing that might come to mind when you think of Japan may be the bold and brazen neon lights of Shibuya, the hustle and bustle of the streets of Shinjuku and the traditional temples of Asakusa. Although these are iconic images of Tokyo, there's so much more richness to Japanese culture that I want to introduce you to. Not the culture shock, but the accessibility, comfort and serenity of it all.

Umai, meaning 'tasty, delicious, appetizing', is a word said with fervour and excitement after that first bite of something that hits the spot. It seemed like a natural title for this book. It was a word I frequently heard after meals I'd make for friends when I moved to Japan, and was the first word that would come out of my mouth when tasting something made with such creativity and mastery that it blew my mind.

There is so much to learn about home-cooked Japanese 'soul food'. Outside Japan, the image of Japanese food tends to be of sushi, lots of raw things, and steaming bowls of ramen – but that's just a small part of the whole picture. This book is about the home-cooked food that families make and grow up on. Japanese culture is so diverse, but it is rooted in food. Every area of the country has different speciality foods they produce or cook, from oysters in Hiroshima to udon noodles in Shikoku. The common thread is that food plays an important role in bringing people together. So often, people show their love and appreciation to their families, partners and friends through the tireless labour of love that goes into cooking for people they care about.

Japanese food has an artistic nature, too. It's very rare to go to someone's house and find just one dish placed in front of you; instead there will be an array of mains, sides, pickles, rice and soup, together displaying a range of tastes, textures and colours. It can be a new way of eating, and this book will be a bit of a hand-hold, imparting essential knowledge to guide you through what to expect if you ever visit Japan. It's a book for those who perhaps already enjoy Japanese food but who might need a helping hand to start cooking it in their own home.

I grew up in London and lived in a household that loved food deeply. Having a Japanese mum and a Spanish-Italian dad meant I regularly got to eat arguably some of the best cuisines, day in, day out. Not just at home (although this was definitely a highlight), but outside too. Londoners are spoilt for choice, with restaurants from innumerable cultures and a merging of cuisines. It's truly a place of fusion, in the best way possible. It was a brilliant city to grow up in, and I was inspired by so many different people and foods.

When I was growing up, we'd visit Tokyo for a month each year, which was the highlight of the summer holidays: long days filled with plenty of delicious food, going to the beach, and lots of ice cream from the local *konbini* (convenience stores). Being a child, I had no responsibilities apart from having fun, so it's no surprise that Japan became my dream destination as a place to live. The naivety of that notion caught up with me when I got a bit older and realized that it's actually not that realistic to move to the other side of the world when you don't speak the language fluently or have any idea what you want to do with your future.

So that plan was parked for a few years until, in a make-or-break moment, I decided to take a two-month trip to Japan.

INTRODUCTION

That journey was to be the decider in whether I made the move to Japan or not. The moment I landed in Tokyo, I knew it was the place I needed to be. I was reminded of how happy I had been in the country: the food, the people, the way of life. It just made sense. I decided to pack up and move, without too much of a plan. I packed two suitcases filled with a few clothes and a bunch of cookbooks and moved to Yokosuka, an hour south of Tokyo, to a house I shared with four skateboarders.

It was an interesting experience, to say the least, but the best part was that I was constantly surrounded by people who were hungry and raring to eat – which made my life a lot easier when I was writing a cookbook. There's nothing more pleasurable than cooking for people who are excited to eat your food and who continuously cheer you on. Of course, all good things must come to an end, and I eventually moved into a quintessential studio apartment in Tokyo: a small 21-square-metre flat that I knew I had to rent as soon as I walked in. It had big windows and, most importantly, the perfect little Japanese kitchen.

Generally, renting an apartment in Japan means zero appliances, but I was lucky enough that this place included a tiny gas stove with enough space to fit two small pans, a tiny grill (broiler) for fish and, right next to it, an area to chop, prepare and plate. I bought a load of IKEA hooks from which to dangle the all-important tea strainer, my mandoline, a chopping board and measuring cups. The fridge, my newfound pride and joy, was the perfect size; it came just up to the height of my shoulders, and I stood on tiptoe to get the microwave oven on top of it. Multi-tasking was now at the forefront of how I cooked: bowls in the sink to hold all the vegetable peels, wiping down the surfaces as I went, and windows left open for as much ventilation as possible so my bed didn't smell like fried chicken by the time I went to sleep.

In many ways, my little kitchen is a reflection of the recipes in this book. Simple dishes that use minimal equipment perfectly encapsulate what *umai* means to me: accessible home cooking that will leave a lasting impression on you and your guests, whether it's a flavour combination you've never tried, or a new technique learned. The recipes are impressive yet have a pared-back approach that anyone can learn.

about this book この本について

This book is separated into four chapters: Easy Lunches, Family Favourites, Izakaya at Home and Desserts. Easy Lunches focuses on intuitive recipes for one or two people. None are particularly challenging, and you'll find most ingredients in a well-stocked pantry (see pages 16–24), with most dishes having a carbohydrate as the main element. I so often find myself cooking for one or two and I wanted to feature recipes that you could make in under 15 minutes.

Family Favourites does what it says on the tin: it's a collection of recipes to cook for a group, for weeknight dinners or easy weekend meals. Many can be made ahead then simply reheated later, and they make excellent leftovers or lunch for the next day. These are all dishes that I grew up on and that I crave when I'm looking for something that reminds me of family. The recipes in this chapter are the ones I get the most requests for when I'm hosting friends in Japan. I guess there's something about someone else cooking dishes from your childhood that feels so sentimental and warming. It goes without saying, but these are, of course, best served with a steaming bowl of rice.

Izakaya at Home is the biggest and possibly the most inspiring chapter. *Izakayas* – the Japanese equivalent of a pub or tavern – have been a huge part of Japanese culture since they started in the seventeenth century. They're all about drinking with friends and loved ones over shared dishes. In this chapter, you'll find Japanese classic recipes to have up your sleeve, such as karaage (fried chicken) and gyoza (pan-fried dumplings), but also some dishes I've tried when travelling around the country. These are generally small plates or dishes designed for sharing.

This is my favourite way to cook and eat, and it is so integral to Japanese life and how people socialize. It seems to be a reoccurring theme that making friends and meeting new people happens during nights at *izakayas*, where people bond over food, drink and having a great night. To channel that *izakaya* buzz, make dinner for two (or more) based on five or six recipes and put on some great music to encourage laughter and chatter.

The Desserts chapter is the most succinct. Japan doesn't have a massive dessert culture, and many recipes have a Western influence, such as Parisian patisserie or Portuguese flan, or German baumkuchen ('tree cake'), which is hugely popular. Many times, dessert means a bite of chocolate, a scoop of ice cream or whatever you can manage to forage from your kitchen. There may be sweet mochi from the local *wagashiya* (traditional Japanese sweet shop), possibly a range of daifuku (mochi filled with sweet red bean paste), kusa mochi (mochi infused with Japanese mugwort leaves) and dango (rice flour dumplings). The treats I've gathered at the end of this book will satisfy anyone with a sweet tooth and will also inspire those who like to bake – and all are super easy to make.

Whichever recipes you decide to cook, I hope you discover new flavour combinations, cooking methods and ingredients to season or flavour the dishes you make, that you can use again and again. After all, cooking is all about being inspired by different cultures – and that's what this book is all about.

ABOUT THIS BOOK

A NOTE ON JAPANESE FLAVOURS

a note on Japanese flavours　日本の味について

Japanese food is all about balance, particularly of sweet and savoury tastes. The main flavouring components tend to be soy sauce, sake, mirin, dashi and sugar. I know the thought of using sugar in savoury dishes may seem surprising, but it's all part of the process, and your dishes will strike the right flavour balance.

One thing you might realize as you read through the recipes is that many Japanese dishes aren't particularly acidic. European cooks so often use a squeeze of lemon or a dash of vinegar to brighten a dish, alongside a pinch of flaky salt to complete it. In Japan, acidic dishes tend to be eaten as a standalone or as part of an *izakaya* spread, rather than added into other dishes in the way gherkins would be added to burgers, for example. Cucumber sunomomo (*sunomono* translates as 'vinegared thing') is a dish you'll come across frequently.

Pickles (tsukemono) are an integral part of Japanese meals but they aren't as strong and intensely vinegary as, say, the pickled cucumbers you'd find in Western supermarkets. They're historically preserved in salt and sometimes rice bran, so the moisture is removed, yet they retain their crunch and some of the fresh flavour. Every vegetable differs, so you'll get the light and crispy kyuri ipponzuke (whole cucumber pickle), and then the polar opposite, umeboshi (pickled plums), which are salted and sun-dried before being slowly fermented, creating an extremely sour and salty pickle that is delicious with rice.

This book is filled with recipes, many of which may be new to you – but think of them as just a starting guide. I truly believe cooking is about intuition above all else. With a bit of experience, you can guesstimate with a soup spoon for a tablespoon or a dessertspoon that doubles as a teaspoon – it's all about trusting your instinct and trying things as you go. Although there are accurate, tested measurements for everything in this book, I hope you will use the recipes as a starting point, and that you will cook a dish more than once, feeling confident enough to substitute or add different ingredients each time. Think of this as a cook's guide to a Japanese kitchen, a portal to creating original, Japanese-inspired recipes with your very own style and signature.

the japanese pantry 日本の食材

There are two keys to being a good cook: be prepared, and have a pantry that's well stocked with essential ingredients. I've compiled a list of the staples you'll need – you will be able to find most of these at your local supermarket or, for something a bit more niche, a Japanese supermarket. There's always the internet, too, and ordering ingredients has never been so easy. See my suppliers list on page 222.

Curry cubes

Japanese curry dishes are a lot milder than their Indian or Thai counterparts, which are typically made with a variety of chillies, spices and herbs. Japanese curry takes its roots from Indian spices, such as cumin, coriander and turmeric, but often blends in sweeter ingredients, such as apples and honey, to form a solid block, or a roux, which forms the basis of the sauce. The resulting sauce is incredibly thick, making it a great vessel for meats and vegetables to be scooped over hot rice. My favourite brands are House Foods Vermont and S&B Torokeru. Both make a good introduction to the flavours of Japanese curry and both are fairly mild. I'm aware that using readymade curry cubes seems like a bit of a cheat, but trust me when I say that no one is going to make curry cubes from scratch when they get back from work – and having these on hand means you can have dinner on the table in 15 minutes. I always have a few secret ingredients up my sleeve to add into my curry to make the flavours richer or spicier, depending on what I feel like.

Hondashi

This indispensable instant stock is one of the main ingredients you'll need in your Japanese pantry. It's the equivalent of the chicken or beef stock you'd buy from the shop but so much better in terms of flavour and ease. Hondashi comes in powdered form and is used in everything from soup bases, hotpots, sauces, okonomiyaki batter (see page 110) and so much more. You'll always find at least two bags in my pantry. It has a deep flavour that is the basis of so much Japanese cooking. It's made with katsuobushi (dried, smoked bonito flakes) and kombu (a type of dried kelp that contains high levels of glutamate and, thus, umami). It's not fishy in the way tinned tuna or sardines are, but it's incredibly smoky and savoury, and it's what gives the dishes that follow their distinct flavour.

For a vegetarian/vegan alternative, you can find great dashi powders made with a base of shiitake mushrooms (my favourite is made by a producer called Kayanoya). The depth of flavour is just as good when substituting vegan dashi in a recipe, although it might be worth adding a touch of smoked salt where possible to recreate the smoky flavour you would otherwise get from bonito flakes.

Kewpie mayonnaise
I couldn't write a Japanese cookbook without mentioning Kewpie mayonnaise. It's my ultimate choice for a mayonnaise, and is what I've used throughout this book. It has a really good balance of flavours, a creamy texture from the egg yolks and a slightly sweeter and zingier taste than many other store-bought brands.

Kirimochi
Kirimochi (cut mochi), shelf-stable cakes made from glutinous rice, are an ingredient to always keep in your pantry. Not to be confused with the sweet, soft mochi eaten as a treat, kirimochi are used in savoury dishes and can be cooked in an instant. They're sold in bags, conveniently individually packaged. Because they have little taste of their own, they're a great vessel for flavour, and they have a delightful chewy texture. In Japan, they are commonly served in dashi with udon, or cooked in a toaster oven or boiled until soft then dipped in soy sauce and wrapped in nori.

Mentaiko
Hailing from Kyushu in western Japan, these sacs of pollock roe are salty and funky, with a slight kick. They're cured for up to a week with salt and chilli (look out for karashi mentaiko for the spicier version). Mentaiko is used in a similar way to how anchovies are used in Italian recipes – served as a standalone dish or used to add a punch of savouriness to dishes that would be hard to obtain otherwise. Look out for the recipe for Mentaiko Pasta (see page 43). It also makes a great addition to potato salad (see Potato Salada on page 178), too.

Mentsuyu
Also called tsuyu, this soy-based dipping sauce for noodles is flavoured with dashi (Japanese stock) and has a touch of sweetness. I love the varieties based on kombu (dried kelp), which are suitable for vegetarians and vegans, but you can find ones with a stronger flavour that are based on dashi made with katsuobushi (dried bonito flakes). Check the label if cooking for vegetarians or vegans. You can find mentsuyu at any Japanese supermarket and it is a good staple to keep in the pantry. As well as being great for seasoning food, it's a lifesaver for those evenings when the last thing you want to do is cook:

Boil your choice of noodles (somen, soba or udon) according to the package instructions. In the meantime, thin out some mentsuyu with water and a pinch of hondashi powder (or vegan alternative; see page 16), and heat it in a small pan.

Crack an egg into a bowl, whisk it, then drizzle it into the simmering menstuyu over a low heat so that long threads of egg cook through the soup, similar to an egg-drop soup. Turn the heat off and let it sit for a couple of minutes.

Drain the noodles, put them in a bowl and top with the egg-drop mentsuyu soup. Done – dinner in five minutes!

Mirin
Mirin is a type of fortified, sweetened sake that's used in so many of the recipes in this book. It's got a high sugar content, which makes it great for making sauces that you want thickened and slightly sweetened. Another great thing to have stocked in your cupboard.

THE JAPANESE PANTRY

Miso

Miso is made by fermenting soybeans with salt and a type of mould called koji. It's a process that goes back centuries. The differences in colour and flavour are generally down to how long it is fermented: a rule of thumb is that the longer it's left, the darker it becomes and the deeper the flavour – although there are other factors such as whether other grains, such as rice and barley, are used. There are countless varieties of miso, but three main types: **Shiro miso** (white miso) is the sweetest and mildest, fermented for a minimum of three months and made with a percentage of rice to create sweetness. This miso is commonly used in dressings, baking and marinades but less so in miso soups where the flavour is too delicate. **Aka miso** (red miso) is fermented for about a year, but can be stored for five to ten years. It is often used in sauces that are balanced with sugar and oil. **Shinshu miso** (brown or yellow miso) is the best of both worlds and the one I always have in my fridge. Barley is normally used to make this miso and it has the saltiness you'd expect from miso, with nuttiness from the grain. This is the miso that's commonly used for miso soups as well as for adding to sauces, such as in Mabo Nasu (see page 96). Miso sold in bags or plastic containers will last in the fridge for a couple of months to a year depending on the type you buy. I always get the type without any dashi added, so I can adjust the seasoning per recipe.

Noodles

There are so many varieties of noodles throughout Japan, but the main ones are udon, soba, somen and ramen. I always keep all four, as well as pasta, in my pantry for speedy meals. **Udon** are the thick, chewy type that hold up super well in broths as well as stir-fried for yakiudon. You'll generally find these sold fresh in the fridge section, or in the freezer section at supermarkets. **Soba** are dried noodles, usually made from a mixture of buckwheat and wheat flour (although you can get gluten-free soba made only with buckwheat). They have a lovely nutty flavour. These can be served cold with mentsuyu and are also delicious with a tahini-based dressing, which complements the flavour so well. **Somen** are super-thin dried wheat noodles and take just a few minutes to cook. **Ramen** noodles, usually sold dried, are made with flour, salt and a specific alkaline water called kansui, which gives them their bouncy texture. They're great to have on hand for noodle soups or for topping with crispy chilli oil, soy sauce and an egg for an easy meal.

Okonomiyaki sauce
Flavour-wise, think of ketchup blended with Worcestershire sauce. Okonomiyaki sauce has a balance of sweet and salty flavours, and will give your dishes a *je ne sais quoi*. It's really just Japan's answer to ketchup, as its always served with fried food or as the base of certain sauces such as the demi-glace sauce typically served with hamburg, the Japanese take on a burger (see Nikomi Hamburg, page 88).

Panko
These dried breadcrumbs are larger and flakier than the fine-ground breadcrumbs that you would use for arancini or a schnitzel, so they create a crunchier crust that's perfect for dishes such as tonkatsu (breaded, fried pork cutlet). In saying this, not all Japanese fried foods use breadcrumbs to achieve a crispy exterior. Often they are made using a light batter – think tempura – or karaage (see page 149), made using flour and potato starch.

Ponzu
A citrus-based sauce made up of vinegar, soy sauce, sugar and a citrus, most commonly a Japanese variety called yuzu. It brightens any dish and can be used in dressings by simply mixing with a bit of extra virgin olive oil, but it is also commonly used as a dipping sauce for nabe, Japanese hotpot.

Rice
Rice is the heart of so much of Japanese cooking and in Japan you'll have a bowl of steaming-hot short-grain rice with at least one meal per day. Koshihikari, a type of short-grain rice, is the main one you'll find in any Asian supermarket and I highly urge you to cook with this rather than long-grain, basmati or jasmine rice when making Japanese food. It's very easy to cook (see page 30) and only takes 12 minutes plus resting time, so there's no need to worry if you don't have a rice cooker.

Rice vinegar
One to have in your pantry, as rice vinegar has a different flavour profile from the other types. The delicate and slightly sweet flavour makes it great for dressings and marinades – as well as for flavouring sushi rice.

Roasted sesame seeds
Rich and nutty, these provide a crunch to finished dishes, as well as flavour. Make sure you look for 'toasted' or 'roasted' sesame seeds on the packaging when buying them (look for them in Japanese grocers or Asian supermarkets). The seeds themselves will also be puffier and slightly darker in colour than raw sesame seeds. In a pinch, you could toast some raw sesame seeds in a dry pan for a few minutes until golden, which will release their wonderful aroma.

The same goes for **toasted sesame oil**, which is always made using roasted sesame seeds to give a glistening and rich finish to many dishes.

Sake
Made from fermented rice, sake is almost the equivalent of using white wine for cooking – but I would say it's used in more recipes and more freely, such as for getting rid of any smells from fish or meat before cooking. There'll always be a litre bottle in any Japanese kitchen. You don't need to cook with expensive sake or anything you'd savour to drink at home, as you'll just be cooking off the alcohol and most of the flavour anyway, so feel free to just buy decent-quality cooking sake.

Seaweed
There are so many types of seaweed that are all used for different purposes, but there are a few that are on constant rotation in my house. **Nori** is the big dog: crispy, crunchy, paper thin – how it's made is an art form in itself. I always have this stocked up for its roasty flavour, to use for *onigiri* (nori-wrapped rice balls) or breaking the sheets up into pieces to serve over rice. **Wakame** is used in miso soup, and a range of different types are used for chilled seaweed salads. **Hijiki** is simmered in a savoury-sweet broth to soak up all the flavours and is eaten as a side dish with rice. **Aonori** is a very fine dried powder that is used to garnish dishes such as okonomiyaki (see page 110) and takoyaki (fried octopus balls). **Kombu** is used for making dashi stock. It is soaked and boiled with katsuobushi for a fragrant and umami rich broth that serves as a base to many Japanese dishes.

Shichimi togarashi
A spice blend from Japan that mixes chilli pepper flakes, sansho pepper flakes, citrus peel, nori, sesame seeds and other dried ingredients. Rather than a sweat-inducing spice, this is more similar to Sichuan pepper, but with a kick of citrus. You would never use this spice blend to marinade or cook with, but it's a great finishing touch on your udon or karaage (see page 149) to give it a little kick.

Shio kombu
This is kelp that is salted and seasoned with soy sauce and sugar, dried and cut into tiny strips. It can be eaten with white rice as a little side dish, but I love using it as an essential flavour-booster in the kitchen, whether it's to make a quick cucumber salad or to add to stir fries. One of my favourite ten-minute meals is to put spaghetti on the boil, finely slice garlic and sweetheart cabbage and fry in a tablespoon of olive oil with a big pinch of shio kombu. A minute before the pasta is done cooking, add a ladleful of pasta water to the cabbage, a pinch of hondashi powder (see page 16) and a few good cracks of black pepper, then add pasta, mix and eat.

Shoyu
This is the Japanese name for soy sauce. Throughout this book I just tend to use the Japanese Kikkoman koikuchi shoyu soy sauce. It's standard, sold everywhere and means you don't need to spend hours looking for light soy sauce, dark soy sauce, and everything in between.

Umeboshi
This salty, sour and sweet plum is not only a great accompaniment to rice but also works brilliantly in dressings to provide a sharp tang. My favourite is hachimitsu umeboshi, which has honey in it, but the other common flavours you can find are shiso, a Japanese herb reminiscent of basil, and katsuobushi, dried, smoked tuna flakes.

The basics

Cooking oils
Neutral oils are your best friend when cooking: you don't want anything with a strong flavour that would distract from the dish. My go-to is rapeseed (canola) oil, but feel free to use sunflower oil or ordinary vegetable oil. Every now and again I'll finish a dish with extra virgin olive oil. I prefer the sweeter, rounded versions over the peppery styles, as they seem to work better with the mild flavours of Japanese cooking. Sesame oil will always be toasted sesame oil and used at the end of cooking or as a finishing drizzle on top (rather than as a cooking oil) to keep the flavour strong and nutty.

Salt
Use fine sea salt for the recipes in this book. You'll mostly find measurements but, if not, just salt to taste. You know your palate the best; some people who eat out a lot often prefer saltier food, and people who cook at home more tend to like things a little lighter. Every now and again, I'll specify finishing a dish with flaky salt for sashimi or steak, but most recipes already have a sauce with the salty, oily flavour we all crave.

Sugar
The standard sugar that is sold in shops in Japan is called jyohakuto. The closest substitute is white caster (superfine) sugar. Although jyohakuto holds a bit more moisture than ordinary caster sugar, the flavour is the same and it's what I use in my recipes.

THE JAPANESE PANTRY

KITCHEN TOOLS

kitchen tools 調理器具

As I mentioned before, Japanese kitchens tend to be small. There's no space for hundreds of gadgets and really there's no need for any of it. I've managed to compact mine into a couple of saucepans, one frying pan (skillet), a good multipurpose knife and a handheld blender that I tuck into the shelves. Graters, scales and mandolines are all great, but optional – they're items I use often, but my recommendations below are for the must haves.

A good knife
It goes without saying, but a good knife really will take you places! Even if you don't have all the extra bits and bobs – such as a mandoline or a food processor – you can definitely get by with a sharp knife. I use a Japanese-style *santoku* (which literally translates to 'three uses') knife, which is a great all-rounder. If you're going to splurge on one item for the kitchen, then I'd recommend a quality *santoku* knife.

Chopsticks
It's worth having several pairs of chopsticks in your kitchen; they're a multipurpose tool. I use them to whisk ingredients together, to stir-fry dishes, and for deep-frying, to transfer and turn food as it cooks. Go for the longer ones, and I recommend plain (unvarnished) wood or bamboo, as they're resistant to heat and won't scratch pans like metal ones do. They are also very useful for testing the temperature of hot oil when deep-frying: put the tip into the hot oil and if a steady stream of air bubbles emerges from the tip, the oil is hot enough to fry.

Hand-held blender/whisk
A magic electronic hand-held blender/whisk is one of the best things I have invested in: it makes your life a hell of a lot easier, whether it's blending soups (you don't need to wait for it to cool as you would with a jug blender), whisking cream or making dressings quickly.

Japanese ceramic or metal graters
A good grater is one of the most useful things you can have in your kitchen: a powerhouse of a tool. A Japanese-style grater is normally circular with a raised area in the middle that has small, protruding nubbins. You can grate garlic and ginger easily on it without nicking your fingers. You can, of course, use a Microplane for recipes that call for grated ginger or garlic, but this is an item to have at the back of your mind if you want an extra kitchen tool. A bonus point is that they're tiny, so they won't take up space on your work surface!

A word on ovens
Very few recipes in this book use an oven, and those that do are in the dessert chapter. This is because most Japanese houses don't have an oven. Instead, there's a small stove made up of two gas hobs with a little grill (broiler) underneath for cooking fish.

the heart of Japanese home cooking 日本の家庭料理のこころ

Home is where the heart is, and a steaming-hot bowl of rice and miso soup will always be ready and waiting for you at the dinner table. The starting point for dinner is typically expressed as とりあえずごはん (toriehzu gohan), or 'First of all, rice' – and dinner plans flow on from that. It's the perfect accompaniment to any meal – breakfast, lunch or dinner.

There's beauty in a bowl of perfectly cooked short-grain white rice, whether it's the makings of a humble solo meal, perhaps topped with umeboshi (salted pickled plums) or natto (fermented soybeans), or as an impressive centrepiece for feeding family and friends. Using a rice cooker will guarantee good results, but I know that many people, including myself, don't own one – and I've learned it's just as easy and a lot quicker to cook it on the stove. All you need is rice, water, a sieve (at a push) and a good cast-iron or non-stick pan.

Rice is the backbone of so many Japanese dishes, so you really don't want to mess it up. The key things to remember are:

- Always, always, always rinse the rice in cold water until it runs as close to clear as possible, to remove a lot of the starch. This should be around five rounds of rinsing.

- Always leave the rinsed rice to soak for 30 minutes before cooking it on the stove. Japanese rice has a short, thick grain – you want the water to soak into it, so you're not left with a crunchy centre to the grain, when cooked.

Miso soup is the heart and soul of any Japanese meal. It's what I crave after being out of the country for too long – the rich and savoury flavours are so warming.

Typically, miso soup is served as a side dish and it's very easy to adjust the ingredients to whatever you may fancy. Seasonal vegetables are perfect for this – my grandma and aunt always made a daikon and white onion version that I was particularly fond of. You could also use the base for a very easy dinner when you want something warming and comforting but still light. I like adding leftover shredded chicken, a handful of vegetables and topping with grilled mochi.

Key
Recipes throughout the book are marked up with the following symbols.

V – vegetarian
VO – vegetarian option
VG – vegan
VGO – vegan option

See also: vegan and vegetarian indexes on pages 234.

steamed rice

gohan

Serves 4

V + VG

285g (10oz/1½ cups) short-grain white rice (ideally Koshihikari, see page 22)

A steaming bowl of rice goes well with just about everything. Even enjoyed on its own it has a slight sweetness and the most satisfying, slightly chewy texture. I generally make a big batch and freeze in portions. Once these are frozen, simply reheat in the microwave for a couple of minutes and you're ready to serve.

Put the rice in a sieve (strainer) and rinse under cold running water. You can be fairly rough in the way you do this, working in circular motions both ways and every so often scrunching the rice to remove as much starch as you can. Rinse and drain the rice 3–5 times until the water runs fairly clear, then drain thoroughly and transfer to a saucepan that has a tight-fitting lid.

Add 400ml (14fl oz/1¾ cups) water to the pan and put the lid on. Let the rice soak in the water for 30 minutes before you start to cook.

With the lid still firmly on, turn the heat to high. When you hear it boiling, turn it down to the lowest heat. Let it simmer for 12 minutes, then turn the heat off.

Keep the lid on for a further 15 minutes, so the rice steams, then take the lid off and mix it gently with a rice paddle or wooden spoon that's been soaked in water.

Serve immediately. If you're not eating it straight away, spread it out on a clean work surface to cool it down quickly, then portion up in cling film (plastic wrap) and store in the fridge for up to 3 days. Alternatively, place in a freezer-safe container and freeze for up to 1 month.

miso soup

miso shiru

Serves 2

VO + VGO

1½ tsp hondashi or vegan alternative (see page 16)

1 tbsp dried wakame seaweed

100g (3½oz) silken tofu, cut into cubes

1 tbsp brown or white miso

You can put just about anything in miso soup. I've opted to write a recipe for a very traditional tofu and wakame (dried seaweed) version, but I also love adding daikon radish and white onion, or making mushroom miso using a type of mushroom called nameko (which you can find in Japanese supermarkets). Its flavour and texture goes so well with the toasty flavours of brown miso.

Put 400ml (14fl oz/1¾ cups) water, the hondashi and wakame in a pan and turn the heat to medium. The wakame will start to rehydrate as the soup cooks.

Bring up to simmering point, then reduce the heat and let it simmer for 3 minutes. Add the tofu and cook for a further 2 minutes.

Turn the heat off and gently whisk in the miso. Serve straight away.

easy lunches

簡単ランチ

It's all too easy to have lunch on the go – a cold sandwich while sitting at your desk, uninspired by the beige that surrounds you. Yet there's something so rewarding about having lunch at a table, away from distractions: you'll taste the flavours, experience the textures and can congratulate yourself for having something nourishing and delicious. Lunch doesn't have to be complicated, nor does it have to take more than 15 minutes. The most time-consuming element in the majority of these recipes will be boiling noodles or cooking rice, which you can easily do in advance if you find yourself in a pinch. These recipes are all about accessibility, about using what you have in your pantry or store cupboard.

    These are dishes I grew up eating. Oyakodon (chicken and egg rice bowl; see page 35) provides so much comfort, it's the equivalent of a hug in a bowl. The recipes for Kabocha Soup (pumpkin soup; see page 47) and Tofu to Buta no Itame (crispy tofu rice bowl with pork; see page 48) are great for packed lunches. The recipes all serve one to two people, but they can easily be doubled and served with side dishes and salads.

34 EASY LUNCHES

chicken and egg rice bowl

oyakodon

Serves 2

VO

3 tbsp soy sauce

2 tbsp mirin

1 tbsp sake

1½ tbsp sugar

150ml (5fl oz/scant ⅔ cup) dashi (150ml/5fl oz/scant ⅔ cup water with 1 tbsp hondashi; see page 16)

½ onion, finely sliced

2 chicken thighs, skin on, cut into bite-sized chunks

3 eggs

To serve

2 servings of hot, steamed rice (see page 30)

finely sliced nori

A family favourite across Japan, this is a 15-minute lunch from the time you take the ingredients out of the fridge to the moment it's steaming and hot on the table. It also uses ingredients you're likely to have to hand. I have such fond memories of my mum making this, and there really is nothing better than an excuse to eat a big bowl of rice served with wobbly eggs flavoured with dashi and tender pieces of chicken.

Feel free to make this vegetarian by substituting tofu for the chicken and be sure to use vegan hondashi. I would recommend using silken tofu or aburaage (fried tofu) and simmering for a couple of minutes in the sauce before adding the eggs. If using silken tofu, be gentle, as it will break apart fairly easily.

Heat the soy sauce, mirin, sake, sugar and dashi in a shallow pan (use one with a lid) over a medium heat. Add the onion and cook for 5 minutes until softened and starting to turn translucent. Add the chicken and cook for 7 minutes with the lid on until the chicken is fully cooked through.

Whisk the eggs in a bowl, then add two-thirds of the eggs to the pan with the chicken and onions. Place the lid on the pan and cook for 2–3 minutes until the eggs are just set, then add the remaining third of the eggs and cook for a further minute so the eggs are half cooked and still jiggly when served.

Spoon the egg and chicken mixture over two bowlfuls of hot rice and top with the nori.

chicken cups with sesame dressing

tori no gomae

Serves 2 as a snack or nibble

100g (3½oz) chicken breast

pinch of salt

1 tbsp sake

½ cucumber, julienned

1 tbsp gari (pickled ginger), or use very finely sliced fresh root ginger

1 small head of butter lettuce

For the roasted sesame dressing

2 tbsp mayonnaise

1½ tbsp toasted sesame seeds

1 tsp neutral oil, such as rapeseed (canola) or sunflower

1 tsp apple cider vinegar

1 tsp soy sauce

1 tsp sugar

1 tbsp water

To serve (optional)

a handful of fresh coriander (cilantro), or other herbs, roughly chopped

2 spring onions (scallions), finely sliced

toasted sesame seeds

Anyone who's spent time in Japan will know the hold that the Kewpie Roasted Sesame Dressing has on local palates. Creamy, slightly tangy, savoury, full of roasted flavours and a little sweet, it's the ideal dressing for absolutely anything. It comes in squeezy bottles and is widely available, but I've created my own version here in case you can't find it. These lettuce cups make a fresh and crunchy snack that serve as a vessel for tender chicken and whatever herbs you have in your fridge.

For the chicken, I've used a microwave for the sake of speed. You'll be surprised at just how much moisture the meat retains when it's cooked this way, and that you're able to cook it in minutes. For those without a microwave, you could poach the chicken or even just use leftover roast chicken or rotisserie chicken.

Slice the chicken lengthways into two long strips and put on a microwave-safe plate. Season with the salt and the sake, then cover with cling film (plastic wrap). Microwave the chicken at 160W for 2½–3 minutes, or until cooked through, then set aside to cool. When cool enough to handle, shred the meat with a fork.

To make the dressing, combine all the ingredients in a bowl and whisk. This will make more dressing than you need, but you can keep it in the fridge for a few days and enjoy with any salad.

Mix the shredded chicken with 3–4 tablespoons of the dressing, the cucumber and gari. Separate the lettuce leaves to make cups and fill them with the chicken mixture. Top with fresh coriander, spring onions and extra toasted sesame seeds to serve, if you like.

EASY LUNCHES

cold ramen

hiyashi chuka

Serves 2

VO

For the sauce

1½ tbsp soy sauce

1½ tbsp rice vinegar

1 tbsp sugar

1 tbsp toasted sesame oil

For the noodles

1 egg

pinch of salt

pinch of sugar

1 tsp neutral oil, such as rapeseed (canola) or sunflower

2 packs of ramen noodles (dry or fresh)

2 slices honey-roast ham, cut lengthways into thin slices

5cm (2in) piece cucumber, cut lengthways into thin slices

1 tbsp dried wakame seaweed (see page 23), rehydrated in 100ml (3½fl oz/scant ½ cup) water, then squeezed dry (optional)

To serve

1 tsp English mustard

toasted sesame seeds

A summer hit that's light and refreshing – exactly what you want when the weather turns warmer. I have fond memories of travelling to Tokyo every summer as a child. The first meal after getting off the plane at Narita Airport and before going to my grandma's house would be hiyashi chuka, often with a side of gyoza dumplings. The thought of cold noodles may seem surprising, but the light, vinegary, refreshing sauce is super easy to slurp up in the heat of August. The dressing works equally well for salads.

I've kept the toppings classic, but feel free to switch it up: chicken or smoked tofu would work nicely here instead of ham. Omit the seaweed if it's hard to find.

To make the sauce, put all the ingredients in a pan along with 1½ tablespoons water, bring to the boil, then reduce the heat and let it simmer for 2 minutes. Take off the heat and set aside to cool.

In the meantime, whisk the egg in a small bowl with a pinch of salt and sugar.

Heat the oil in a frying pan (skillet), then add the egg mixture in one thin layer, like a crêpe or thin omelette. Cook for 2 minutes on one side, then carefully flip and cook for 1 minute on the other side. Remove from the pan and slice into thin strips.

Cook the noodles according to the package instructions, then rinse under cold running water and divide between two plates. Top with the omelette and ham slices, cucumber and wakame. Drizzle the sauce around the edges and serve with a dab of mustard to the side of each plate and a sprinkle of toasted sesame seeds.

EASY LUNCHES

marinated tuna rice bowl

zuke maguro don

Serves 2

2½ tbsp soy sauce

2 tbsp sake

1 tbsp mirin

1 tsp toasted sesame oil

150g (5½oz) raw tuna, diced into 2cm (¾in) cubes

To serve

2 servings of hot, steamed rice (see page 30)

2 egg yolks

a handful of finely sliced nori

1 tbsp toasted sesame seeds

5cm (2in) piece of myoga, finely sliced, or finely sliced fresh root ginger

2 shiso leaves (a Japanese herb reminiscent of basil), finely sliced (optional)

handful of chives, finely chopped (optional)

This is a bit of a luxury lunch, but if you're looking for something special that's still very easy, this is the recipe for you. It's incredibly impressive for something that takes just 10 minutes and really is only a handful of ingredients thrown together. For a dish as simple as this, you want to use the best ingredients.

Myoga is a type of Japanese ginger. It has the same sharpness as fresh root ginger but with a hint of citrus zest. It's delicious when thinly sliced raw over fish dishes.

Put the soy sauce, sake, mirin and sesame oil in a small pan and bring to the boil. Cook for 1 minute to burn off some of the alcohol, then remove from the heat and set aside to cool.

When the marinade is completely cool, add the diced tuna, stir to combine and set aside to marinate for 10 minutes.

To serve, put the hot rice in serving bowls, then top with the marinated tuna and nestle an egg yolk into the centre of each portion. Scatter over the nori and sesame seeds and finish the bowls with the myoga, shiso and chives if using.

Note: People with compromised immune systems are advised to avoid raw eggs.

EASY LUNCHES

EASY LUNCHES

spaghetti with spicy cod's roe

mentaiko pasta

Serves 2

150g (5½oz) spaghetti

50g (1¾oz) mentaiko (spicy cod's roe; see page 18)

5 tbsp double (heavy) cream

1 tbsp soy sauce

½ tsp freshly ground black pepper

½ tsp chilli flakes

2 tsp butter

1 sheet of nori, sliced into thin strips, to serve

Don't knock it until you try it. Spicy cod's roe in a creamy sauce with pasta is a Japanese staple. You'll find packets of cod's roe sauce in every supermarket, but it's so easy to make at home, and that's the way we've always done it. My mum's a big fan of a simple buttery mentaiko spaghetti, but I love the way the cream makes the sauce cling onto each strand of pasta. The sauce works super well with thick, chewy udon noodles, too.

Boil the pasta according to the package instructions.

Meanwhile, mix the mentaiko, cream, soy sauce, black pepper and chilli flakes in a large bowl and set aside.

Once the pasta is cooked, drain, saving 2 ladlefuls of the cooking water. Add 1 ladleful of the pasta water to the sauce in the bowl.

Melt the butter in a pan, then add the pasta, followed by the sauce, turning off the heat immediately and mixing vigorously. Add some of the remaining pasta water if you need to loosen it. Sprinkle the nori on top and serve immediately.

simmered fried-tofu udon

kitsune udon

Serves 2

V + VG

For the aburaage

2 tbsp soy sauce

2 tbsp sugar

Two 16 x 8cm (6¼ x 3¼in) pieces of aburaage (fried tofu pockets)

For the udon and broth

700ml (24fl oz/3 cups) dashi (700ml/24fl oz/3 cups water mixed with 2½ tbsp hondashi or vegan alternative, see page 16)

3 tbsp mentsuyu (see page 18); ensure it is vegan, if necessary

1 large leek, sliced on an angle into 1cm (½in) pieces

2 packs fresh udon noodles (350g/12oz total weight)

2 bunches spinach (40g/1½oz)

Kitsune udon is found in every udon shop around the country, whether you're at a sit-down restaurant or a train-station platform. The best types are those where the fried tofu is deeply soaked in the sweet broth and placed as a large piece on top of hot udon. I add greens: the sweetness of the leeks are so delicious when simmered in dashi, adding more flavour to the soup, and I add spinach just because I love it. You could also add green beans, or finely sliced asparagus would work well in the spring. This one's definitely a crowd-pleaser for all ages. Kids love the sweet simmered tofu and the slurpability of the udon.

Aburaage, fried tofu pockets, are a popular ingredient. You'll find them in the fridge or freezer section of Japanese markets. They're used in miso soups, hotpots, inari sushi (rice stuffed into a sweet tofu pocket) and kitsune udon. If you can't find aburaage, you can use atsuage (thick fried tofu) by slicing it into 1.5cm (⅝in) cubes.

Heat 3½ tablespoons water, the soy sauce and sugar in a small pan over a high heat until boiling, then reduce the heat, submerge the aburaage in the liquid and simmer for 7 minutes. When it's done, it should be darker in colour and will have absorbed most of the liquid. Remove and set aside.

Meanwhile, for the broth, mix the dashi and mentsuyu in a pan over a medium heat until simmering, then add the leek. Cook for 5 minutes, or until the leek is soft, then add the noodles and cook for a further 3 minutes. Turn off the heat, add the spinach and leave to wilt for 30 seconds.

To serve, divide the noodles between two bowls, top with the vegetables and a piece of aburaage for each bowl, then ladle over the broth.

EASY LUNCHES

pumpkin soup

kabocha soup

Serves 4

V + VGO

1 tbsp neutral oil, such as rapeseed (canola) or sunflower

½ white onion (100g/3½oz), finely chopped

500g (1lb 2oz) kabocha squash, peeled and cut into 5cm (2in) cubes

400ml (14fl oz/1¾ cups) vegetable stock

100ml (3½fl oz/scant ½ cup) milk

salt and freshly ground black pepper, to taste

2 tbsp double (heavy) cream, to serve (optional)

The simplest of soups but oh-so-nostalgic and delicious, so creamy and warming. Kabocha, with its rough green skin and dense, sweet, orange flesh, really is the only type of squash you can use for this soup as it's wonderfully sweet and nutty. If you can't find it, you could use acorn squash – or overhaul the recipe altogether and use sweetcorn as a substitute to make a creamy sweetcorn soup – another Japanese favourite that you'll find in the hot-food vending machines in Japanese cities over winter.

You could make this vegan by using soy milk instead of milk.

Heat the oil in a large pan, then add the onion and sauté, adding a generous pinch of salt, for 5 minutes, or until softened and translucent. Throw in the kabocha, stir it a few times, then add the stock and simmer for 15 minutes, or until the kabocha is completely softened. Let it cool slightly, then blend using a hand-held blender until smooth.

Put the soup back on the heat, stir in the milk, add black pepper to taste and simmer until warmed through. Serve immediately with some cream stirred through, if you like.

EASY LUNCHES

crispy tofu rice bowl with pork

tofu to buta no itame

Serves 2

250g (9oz) firm tofu

3 tbsp neutral oil, such as rapeseed (canola) or sunflower

100g (3½oz) pork mince (ground pork)

1 red or green capsicum (bell pepper), finely sliced

1 tbsp oyster sauce

1 tbsp soy sauce

1 tbsp sake

1 garlic clove, finely grated

1 tsp toasted sesame oil

½ tsp hondashi (see page 16)

This came about as a throw-together lunch and it ended up turning into quite the lunch classic in my household. It's super savoury and has a variety of textures running throughout. The tofu gets crispy and browned on the outside while the middle stays nice and jiggly, and the browned pork serves as a supporting character, so it's not too heavy on the meat. Capsicums (bell peppers) work well, but it would be quite easy to sub in any veg you like, although I'd recommend something robust to stand up to the rest of the dish rather than leafy greens.

Pat the tofu dry with paper towels and put on a plate with a weight (such as a frying pan/skillet) on top for 30 minutes–1 hour. Once much of the water has been pressed out, slice the tofu into 8–10 even pieces.

Heat the oil in a pan. When hot, add the tofu and fry it, in batches if needed, for 3 minutes per side until browned and crispy all over. Do not touch the tofu until you can see the underside going brown, as this is the star of the show! Once cooked, set the tofu aside on paper towels to soak up any excess oil while you prepare the rest of the dish.

Reheat the oil left in the pan and fry the pork mince, stirring. When bits are getting nicely browned, add the pepper slices and cook for just 3 minutes – you want them to retain vibrancy and a bit of crunch.

Add the oyster sauce, soy sauce, sake, grated garlic, sesame oil and hondashi to the pan, stir and let the flavours come together. Add the tofu at the end and mix gently so the pieces don't break. Serve with rice.

EASY LUNCHES

EASY LUNCHES

EASY LUNCHES

cold chilli-oil soba noodles

hiyashi rayu soba

Serves 2

100g (3½oz) chicken breast

1 tsp salt

1 tbsp sake

125g (4½oz) soba noodles

2 spring onions (scallions), finely sliced

½ sheet of nori, cut into thin strips

1 tbsp toasted sesame seeds

For the dipping sauce

2 tbsp mentsuyu (see page 18)

2 tbsp your favourite crispy chilli oil (I love Momoya's Taberu Rayu)

1 tbsp crispy fried onions

2 very fresh eggs

This recipe is inspired by a favourite dish from a restaurant (now sadly closed) called Fujisawa in Yokosuka, where I used to live. I was served it in the heat of October, the day before my return flight to London. Light, fresh, filled with flavour and punch, it is engrained in my memory and was something I came to crave whenever I returned. This is my ode to the dish that made getting on a 15-hour flight back to Japan so worthwhile and delicious.

For the chicken, I've used a microwave for the sake of speed. You'll be surprised at just how much moisture the meat retains when it's cooked this way, and that you're able to cook it in a mere 5 minutes. For those without a microwave, you could poach the chicken or even just use leftover roast chicken or rotisserie chicken. A scattering of lightly blanched green beans and sugar snap peas would be a welcome bright addition, if you like.

I recommend always having a jar of crispy chilli oil in the pantry or store cupboard, and I'm a strong disciple of Momoya's Taberu Rayu. It has plenty of crispy garlic, onions and sesame seeds, and is not too spicy. Find one you like (there are plenty on the market), but be aware that some, such as the more fragrant, Chinese-influenced Lao Gan Ma, will change the final flavour, so adjust accordingly.

Slice the chicken breast lengthways into two long strips and put on a microwave-safe plate. Season with the salt and the sake, cover with cling film (plastic wrap) and microwave at 160W for 2½–3 minutes, or until cooked through. Set the chicken aside to cool slightly while you prepare the rest of the dish. When it's cool enough to handle, shred the chicken with a fork.

Boil the soba noodles for 5 minutes, or according to the package instructions, then rinse under cold running water and divide between two plates or bowls.

To make the dipping sauce, mix the mentsuyu with the crispy chilli oil and 5–6 tablespoons of water. Divide between two small bowls and top with the crispy fried onions. Crack each egg into separate small bowls.

To serve, top the soba with a generous amount of shredded chicken, spring onions, nori and toasted sesame seeds, and serve the dipping sauce and the raw eggs in their bowls alongside.

Halfway through eating, whisk the raw egg with your chopsticks and add it into the dipping sauce to enjoy the different flavour it gives when you dip the noodles into it.

Note: People with compromised immune systems are advised to avoid raw eggs.

marinated tomato somen

tomato no marine no somen

Serves 2

V + VG

For the marinated tomatoes

150g (5½oz) cherry tomatoes

½ spring onion (scallion), finely sliced

2 tbsp soy sauce

1 tsp toasted sesame oil

½ tsp sugar

1 garlic clove, finely grated

For the somen and dipping sauce

100g (3½oz) somen noodles

2 tbsp mentsuyu (see page 18); vegan, if necessary

2 tbsp tenkasu (optional)

A few years back, my mum made these marinated tomatoes that were full of sweetness and punch, elevating my favourite snack to new heights. These marinated tomatoes are great on their own or tossed through a salad with mozzarella, but I also found that they made a wonderful accompaniment to chilled somen noodles served with a sauce for dipping. Make the tomatoes in the morning and they'll be perfect by lunchtime.

Tenkasu are crunchy bits of fried tempura batter, which you sprinkle on top of noodle dishes for a bit of extra crunch. You can find them in Japanese supermarkets.

Wash the tomatoes and make a small incision in the skin at the bottom of each one. Bring a pan of water to the boil, add the tomatoes and boil them for 1 minute. Drain and immediately plunge them in a bowl of cold water. Gently peel away the skins.

Mix all the remaining marinade ingredients in a jar or glass bowl, adding 2 tablespoons of cold water to combine, then add the tomatoes. Give them a shake and leave them in the fridge, covered, for a minimum of 3 hours.

When you're ready to eat, cook the somen noodles in boiling water for 2–3 minutes, then rinse under cold water. Combine the mentsuyu with 5 tablespoons of water and divide between two small bowls.

Divide the drained noodles between two bowls, top with a generous serving of the marinated tomatoes and the tenkasu, if using. Serve with the sauce on the side for dipping the noodles.

EASY LUNCHES

EASY LUNCHES

grilled mochi

yaki mochi

Serves 2 as a snack

V

2 kirimochi (see page 18)
1 tbsp soy sauce
2 slices sharp cheddar
1 sheet of nori, halved

This isn't so much a recipe, but more a tip on how to create the most wonderful mid-afternoon snack you could ask for. Don't worry about exact measurements – see this is as more about the ingredients that are delicious when put together. I eat this for breakfast, lunch, evening: it's an anytime hand-held snack.

Preheat the grill (broiler). When hot, place the mochi under it and cook for 3–4 minutes per side, turning carefully. They should puff up and go slightly brown in some areas.

Once the outsides are crunchy and the insides look soft and chewy, crush the mochi lightly and dip both sides in soy sauce. Place each cheese slice on a sheet of nori and wrap around the mochi. Serve steaming hot.

EASY LUNCHES

EASY LUNCHES

octopus and tomato pasta

taco to tomato no pasta

Serves 2

150g (5½ oz) spaghetti

2 tbsp olive oil

2 garlic cloves, lightly crushed with the back of a knife

½ tsp chilli flakes

150g (5½oz) cherry tomatoes, halved

2 tbsp sake

1 tbsp soy sauce

100g (3½oz) octopus, pre-boiled and cut into bite-sized pieces

2 tsp butter

salt

This is a quick, 10-minute recipe, but it requires constant stirring and attention to make sure nothing overcooks, so read the recipe through and have all the ingredients measured, prepped and ready to go before getting stuck in.

This beautifully summery dish highlights all the best produce and combines Japanese flavours with Italian techniques. I'd recommend getting a pack of ready-cooked and prepared octopus (with no extra seasoning), so you don't have to go to the effort of cooking octopus at home.

Bring a large pan of salted water to the boil, add the pasta and cook for 2 minutes less than the time stated on the package. Drain and set aside. While it's cooking, ladle off some of the cooking water and set aside to use in the sauce later.

Meanwhile, heat the olive oil in a large sauté pan over a medium heat. When hot, add the garlic and chilli flakes, stirring. After a couple of minutes, the garlic should become fragrant, which will be your cue to add the cherry tomatoes. Let this sauce simmer, stirring to prevent sticking, for 5 minutes until the tomatoes are nice and jammy, then stir in the sake and soy sauce.

Once some of the alcohol has evaporated (1–2 minutes), add the octopus and let it heat through for 2 minutes, making sure it doesn't overcook. This is the point that everything is done almost at once, so add your drained pasta and a dash of pasta water along with the butter and mix vigorously until glossy. Serve immediately on a large, warmed platter.

prawn and dashi pasta

ebi to dashi no pasta

Serves 2

150g (5½oz) linguine

2 tbsp olive oil

½ onion, finely diced

2 garlic cloves, finely sliced

1 tsp chilli flakes

400g (14oz) can cherry tomatoes

1 tsp hondashi (see page 16)

3½ tbsp single (light) cream

200g (7oz) peeled raw prawns (shrimp)

1 tbsp butter

salt and freshly ground black pepper

To serve

15g (½oz) parsley, finely chopped

finely grated Parmesan (Parmigiano Reggiano), to serve

I love a prawn (shrimp) pasta as much as the next person, whether it's with a garlicky olive oil sauce or cloaked in a rich tomato sauce. I created this Japanese-inflected dish to amp it to another level, being quite generous with the dashi, which adds a deep, smoky flavour to the sauce. It's extremely comforting. If you're gluten free, the sauce would be delicious served on top of polenta.

Bring a large pan of salted water to the boil, add the linguine and cook for 2 minutes less than the time stated on the package. Drain and set aside. While it's cooking, ladle off some of the cooking water and set aside to use in the sauce later.

Meanwhile, heat the olive oil in a large sauté pan over medium heat. When hot, add the onion and garlic, season with salt and cook, stirring, for 5 minutes until the onion is softened, then stir in the chilli flakes.

Add the tomatoes, hondashi and cream along with 3½ tablespoons of the pasta water, season with salt and pepper, and let it all simmer for 10 minutes, stirring occasionally. Add the prawns for the final 2–3 minutes, cooking until pink and plump.

Add the drained pasta, a ladleful of the pasta water and butter to the pan, then mix thoroughly to combine.

Serve on a large warmed platter with a scattering of parsley and a grating of Parmesan.

EASY LUNCHES

EASY LUNCHES

chicken and lotus root pasta

tori to renkon no pasta

Serves 2

1 tbsp olive oil

150g (5½ oz) chicken mince (ground chicken)

2 garlic cloves, crushed

65g (2¼oz) renkon (lotus root), quartered and finely sliced (optional)

50g (1¾oz) maitake (hen of the wood) mushrooms or shiitake mushrooms, torn

150ml (5fl oz/scant ⅔ cup) single (light) cream

1 tbsp soy sauce

30g (1oz) Parmesan (Parmigiano Reggiano), finely grated, plus extra to serve

250g (9oz) fresh tagliatelle pasta

salt and freshly ground black pepper

This dish is inspired by an Italian restaurant in Yokosuka, where I used to live. I'm always so inspired by their Japanese takes on international dishes, incorporating things like burdock root and minced (ground) pork into pasta sauces. This is my ode to a dish I loved that's no longer on their menu, but that I now cook at home. You can leave the lotus root out of the recipe if it's too hard to find; it will work well with just chicken and mushrooms.

Start by making the sauce. Heat the olive oil in a large sauté pan over a medium-low heat. When hot, add the chicken mince and a pinch of salt and cook, stirring, until browned. Add the crushed garlic, renkon, if using, and the mushrooms, seasoning generously with salt and pepper. Cook for 4–5 minutes, stirring, then add the cream, soy sauce and Parmesan.

While the sauce is cooking, bring a large pan of salted water to the boil. When the sauce is almost finished, add the pasta to the water and cook for 2–3 minutes. Quickly drain the pasta and add it directly to the sauce in the pan with a ladleful of pasta water to loosen it. Stir well and serve immediately with extra Parmesan.

rice balls

onigiri

Serves 2

VO + VGO

300g (10½oz) freshly cooked rice

1½ tbsp furikake (a savoury Japanese dried seasoning for rice made with seaweed, sesame seeds, and dried fish) (optional)

2 sheets of nori

salt

Choice of fillings

umeboshi (salted plums; see page 24)

tuna mayo

mentaiko (spicy cod's roe; see page 18)

You can make onigiri as simple or as exciting as you please. I have to say my favourite has always been tuna mayo whether it's been made at home or bought from the local 7-Eleven on the way home from a late night. For the vegetarians, fill with umeboshi and use shio kombu (see page 23) in place of furikake.

This simple rice ball, perfectly salted with a crispy sheet of nori on the outside, is a source of deep nostalgia and comfort. In a scene in the classic animated film *Spirited Away*, the young protagonist, Chihiro, when given this simple snack, gets teary-eyed about how delicious something so simple can be.

If using furikake or shio kombu, mix it into the rice while still hot, rather than serving as a chunk in the middle of the onigiri, so the flavour is evenly distributed.

Wet your hands and sprinkle a bit of salt on them so the rice will be seasoned as you shape it. Take a handful of rice in your left hand and cup it, pressing the centre in slightly to form a hollow, then add your filling of choice. Top this with some extra rice and push it all together with your hands so you're cupping around both sides of the rice.

Create a spherical shape with your hand and rotate the rice around while pressing it down slightly; this will keep it compact but not too dense. To give it the classic triangular shape, cup both hands into a 'V' shape and gently mould the rice into shape. Keep your hands slightly damp so the rice doesn't get stuck to them.

Finally, dry your hands thoroughly and wrap the outside of each onigiri in a sheet of nori. Roll the edges of the onigiri in furikake if you want to impress your guests. Serve immediately.

EASY LUNCHES 65

grilled rice balls

yaki onigiri

Serves 2

V + VGO

300g (10½oz) freshly cooked rice (see page 30)

1 tbsp soy sauce

1 tsp mirin

1 tsp hondashi or vegan alternative (see page 16)

1 tsp sesame seeds

a drizzle of toasted sesame oil

55g (2oz) grated mozzarella or mozzarella and cheddar blend (vegetarian, if necessary)

A bonus recipe for those that have mastered the simple onigiri (see page 64) – these are often served at barbecues at the end of the meal and have a nice roasted flavour. I add some cheese to the centre for an untraditional but very delicious twist, but you could keep them plain or use any fillings of your choice. Think of it as a handheld version of the crunchy rice that you get on the bottom of Korean bibimbap or other dishes where rice gets cooked until it's crunchy and delicious.

Mix the rice with the soy sauce, mirin, hondashi, sesame seeds and toasted sesame oil and shape into onigiri, following the instructions on page 64, omitting the nori. Fill each with a cube of the cheese.

Preheat the grill (broiler) or get a non-stick pan hot on the hob.

Once shaped, cook the onigiri under the grill for 1 minute on each side (or fry in a dry non-stick pan for 3 minutes on each side) until browned and starting to crisp.

Serve while still hot, being careful of the molten cheese.

chicken katsu sandwich

tori katsu sando

Serves 2

For the chicken

250g (9oz) skinless, boneless chicken thigh fillets (4 thighs)

30g (1oz) plain (all-purpose) flour seasoned with a pinch of salt

1 egg

40g (1½oz) panko breadcrumbs

4 tbsp neutral oil, such as rapeseed (canola) or sunflower

1 tbsp shichimi togarashi (see page 23)

1 tsp toasted sesame seeds

flaky salt

For the sandwich

4 slices thick white bread, crusts removed

2 tsp softened butter

1 tbsp tonkatsu sauce (I use Bulldog)

1 tbsp mayonnaise

30g (1oz) cabbage, finely sliced

This Japanified club sandwich has become one of the country's iconic dishes. Crispy, crunchy, the perfect amount of saucy, it's a sandwich that satisfies all tastes. You can find it at the local *konbini* (convenience store) to grab on your way out, or in upscale dining establishments, made using the best-quality meats and fried to perfection.

This sandwich is easily in my top three recipes. It's inspired partly by being a child and always looking forward to going to a restaurant called Maisen Aoyama in Tokyo (see page 70) and ordering the pork sandwich – an undulterated juicy pork loin that was deep fried in house-made panko breadcrumbs and sandwiched between thick slices of Japanese shokupan bread (see page 217), which has a brioche-like sweetness (it's enriched with milk and butter), with a lick of tangy tonkatsu sauce. I've kept this sandwich simple, with minimal accoutrements. Just trust the simplicity – and, it goes without saying, cut off the bread crusts.

Put the chicken thighs between two sheets of baking paper and, using a rolling pin, flatten to 1.5–2cm (⅝–¾in) thick.

Create a breading station: put the seasoned flour in one bowl, whisk the egg in a separate bowl, and put the panko breadcrumbs on a plate. Dip the flattened chicken pieces first in the flour, then the egg, followed by the panko.

Heat the oil in a shallow frying pan (skillet) over a medium-high heat. After 4 minutes or so, it should be hot enough. To test: dip the tip of a wooden or bamboo chopstick into the oil. When a steady stream of small air bubbles form and rise to the surface, it's ready to fry with.

Fry the chicken pieces until golden brown and cooked through, 2–3 minutes on each side. Once cooked, transfer the chicken to a plate lined with paper towels to drain away excess oil, and immediately sprinkle with a generous amount of shichimi togarashi, sesame seeds and flaky salt.

Get the bread ready by buttering one side of each piece of bread. Spread the bottom slices of bread with the tonkatsu sauce, then the mayonnaise, then add the chicken. Top with the cabbage and the remaining bread. Serve as is or cut in half.

EASY LUNCHES

EASY LUNCHES

EASY LUNCHES

a love letter to Maisen   まいせんのラブレター

There was no way I could write this book without mentioning one of my favourite restaurants in the world; a place that I've visited time and time again since I was a child and one of my earliest food memories. Maisen is a tonkatsu restaurant in the centre of Tokyo, just off the luxury streets of Omotesando on a quaint road with little boutiques and hairdressers. They specialize in deep-fried pork cutlet – the Japanese equivalent of a schnitzel, but a lot thicker than its European counterpart.

Walk through the winding streets of Aoyama and, the closer you get to it, you'll find a sign pointing to Maisen. The restaurant opens at 11a.m., and by 11:15a.m., rain or shine, there's already a queue around the corner. Previously a public bathhouse built in the 1920s that was renovated, this *tonkatsu-ya* has been open for sixty years. As you walk in there is intimate counter seating for 15 people, ready for those single diners that are in and out for lunch, where you can watch the chefs effortlessly frying the pork cutlet in front of you. You'll spot salarymen, women on a little shopping break and children with their legs dangling off the seats as they eat their katsu sandwiches.

Beautiful Eames-style black leather and wooden chairs fill the dining room. Its high ceilings and dark beams give the restaurant a modern feel in contrast to the traditional building and the neutral colour scheme creates a homey, yet still open, vibe. Natural light floods into the main dining room, where you can hear the buzz and chatter of the lunch rush. Every part of the experience is designed to excite your senses.

Waitresses wear fitted retro pinafores with crisp white shirts and bandanas to keep their hair back while trotting around the restaurant. As they seat you, you'll immediately be presented with a small serving of daikon oroshi (finely grated daikon) with a sprinkling of smoky katsuobushi (dried smoked bonito flakes) to be drizzled with a touch of soy sauce to whet your appetite before the meal. It makes a light counterpart to the warm houjicha, a dark roasted green tea, you sip on as you browse the menu.

There's no way you go to Maisen without ordering tonkatsu, which comes in different cuts to suit personal tastes. Black pork is on the menu for those who prefer a fattier cut, and for the leaner counterpart look out for the hirekatsu or pork loin. Each piece is tenderized before frying, so even the smaller cuts are extremely juicy.

Maisen manages the perfect balance, so each bite of the freshly fried exterior of the tonkatsu is crisp and light – with not a touch of oil coming off it – while the inside remains tender. There are no corners cut when it comes to the dish: even the shokupan bread is baked in-house every morning and shredded into thick panko (breadcrumbs) to coat the meat. A touch of sweetness in the brioche-style loaf provides a harmonious balance in each bite.

Served with the cutlet is tonkatsu sauce, an invention from Japan of brown sauce made with fruits and vegetables, namely apples, prunes, celery and carrots. It is savoury, sweet, tangy and rich. On the table, there are also two clay pots where you can choose from amakuchi (a sweeter, thicker sauce) or karakuchi (similar to Worcestershire sauce) for drizzling over the tonkatsu. Simmered for days, the flavours of the sauces are incredibly deep and rich, both providing a slight tang and savoury taste to each bite.

It may not seem very exciting, but sliced cabbage is also an essential part of the meal. The waiters and waitresses walk around the room with an icy bowl filled to the brim with sliced cabbage for whenever anyone wants a refill. The the extremely crisp, cold cabbage, sliced half a millimetre thick and piled up high, cuts through the richness of the meat. It can be topped with their sesame dressing for when you want something thicker and creamier or the light ponzu dressing brings a citrussy touch.

The small salty addition of otsukemono (pickled vegetables) similarly helps cut through the richness of the main event. Chinese cabbage is pickled, but not in the manner of a vinegared, astringent pickle. Instead, it is lightly salted and preserved with a small amount of yuzu peel. Eaten atop rice as a palate cleanser, they make an especially good way to end your meal.

No dessert is needed when a meal is this balanced. Quite frankly, perfection is the only word for it.

EASY LUNCHES

aubergine katsu sandwich

nasu katsu sando

Serves 2

V + VGO

For the slaw

2 tbsp mayonnaise

1 tsp grainy (wholegrain) mustard

1 tsp apple cider vinegar

½ tsp honey

¼ head of cabbage, finely sliced

1 cucumber, finely sliced

salt to taste

For the sandwich

2 tbsp plain (all-purpose) flour

50g (1¾oz) panko breadcrumbs

1 aubergine (eggplant), finely sliced

100ml (3½fl oz/scant ½ cup) neutral oil, such as rapeseed (canola) or sunflower

smoked salt, or regular flaked salt

1 tbsp toasted sesame seeds

2 burger buns, sliced in half

2 tsp butter

okonomiyaki sauce, to taste (see page 22)

Inspired by the classic katsu sando, I made a lighter version with aubergine (eggplant), which is still full of meaty texture and flavour. It's crunchy, filled with a well-dressed slaw and topped with okonomiyaki sauce. I serve this in buns, so I guess it's actually more of a burger than a sandwich but, either way, it's delicious. Another bonus is that it only requires a shallow fry, so you don't need to worry about wasting a whole lot of oil or your kitchen smelling. To make this vegan, omit the butter, use vegan mayo and add a touch of sugar in place of the honey in the slaw.

For the slaw, combine the mayonnaise, mustard, apple cider vinegar and honey in a bowl. Stir well, then toss through the cabbage and cucumber and season with salt. Set aside.

In a shallow bowl, whisk the flour and 4 tablespoons of water to make a batter. Put the panko breadcrumbs in a second shallow bowl. Coat the aubergine slices in the batter, then dust in the panko until fully coated. Set aside on a plate until all the slices are well coated.

Now you can start frying. Heat the oil in a shallow pan over a medium-high heat. After 3–4 minutes, it should be hot enough. To test: dip the tip of a wooden or bamboo chopstick into the hot oil. When a steady stream of small air bubbles form and rise to the surface, it's ready to fry with.

Fry the aubergine slices for 2 minutes on each side until golden, then transfer to a plate lined with paper towels to drain away excess oil. Sprinkle with smoked salt and sesame seeds while still hot.

To assemble your sandwich, toast and butter the buns, then layer the bottom buns with the slaw, a few aubergine slices and a dash of okonomiyaki sauce. Top with the bun tops and eat immediately. The messier, the better.

smoked mackerel and egg udon

saba tama udon

Serves 2

¼ white onion, finely sliced

1 egg

2 smoked mackerel fillets

2 packs fresh udon noodles (350g/12oz in total)

handful of rocket (arugula) leaves, to serve

For the dashi broth

2 tbsp hondashi (see page 16)

1 tbsp soy sauce

This recipe is a bit of a hidden gem. I've seen it made many times with canned sardines or mackerel and an onsen tamago ('hot spring egg' – an egg that's been cooked in its shell at a low temperature), but this is my spin on it. I love the oiliness of smoked mackerel and that's just one of two components that need heating in this recipe. It is very easy to put together and always reminds me of spring. The dashi broth adds a welcome warmth and light flavour, but you could add a spoon of chilli oil or crispy chilli oil to make it a bit punchier; the udon and mackerel will hold up incredibly well to it.

Soak the sliced onion in a small bowl of iced water while you prepare the rest of the recipe.

Bring a pan of water to the boil and boil the egg for 6½ minutes exactly, then plunge it into iced water to prevent further cooking. This will give you an egg with a firm white and a jammy yolk. When cool enough to handle, peel, then slice the egg in half just before serving.

Preheat the oven to 160° fan/180°C/350°F/Gas mark 4 and cook the smoked mackerel for 10 minutes until heated through and the skin is crisped up.

For the dashi broth, heat 800ml (28fl oz/3¼ cups) water, the hondashi and soy sauce in a pan over a medium heat until it just reaches simmering point.

While the broth is cooking, bring another pan of water to the boil, cook the udon for 3 minutes, then drain.

To serve, divide the udon between two bowls, pour over the dashi broth, top each with a smoked mackerel fillet and a boiled egg half. Scatter over the rocket leaves and add a pinch of icy cold, finely sliced onion.

EASY LUNCHES

the lunch noodle　お昼の立ち食い

There's no way you'll catch a local eating a sandwich on the way back from a *konbini* (convenience store) on their lunch break or eating crisps on the go. Eating while walking is pretty frowned upon in Japan – but there really is such a thing as a 15-minute lunch. You'll find the holy trifecta of a workday lunch – speed, value and taste – at what's known as a *tachigui* (standing restaurant).

There's a surprisingly big culture of standing restaurants in Japan – they're less a full-on restaurant experience and more a place to pop in and have a bite, whether you're on a train platform for a bite of udon at lunch or going to a *tachinomi* (standing *izakaya*) on a small side street at night.

You'll be met with a 'ding ding ding' of wind chimes when you walk into a *tachigui* filled with locals, and probably a queue if it's somewhere extra special. From salarymen to students, you'll see them all standing side by side slurping on noodles.

But before we get to the eating experience, let's go back a few steps. You'll normally be greeted by a large machine: sometimes overwhelming with its array of Japanese characters, a few blue buttons and a few red buttons. 'What does this even mean?', I hear you ask. You'll usually find a selection of hot noodles (red) and cold noodle dishes (blue, obviously). And, yes, you can of course whip out Google Translate and check what each one means – or just take a lucky dip and click on one button, pay (normally cash only in these kind of spots), grab your ticket and give it to the person behind the counter. Within a mere three minutes, you'll be handed a big bowl of comfort: udon noodles in a steaming hot dashi broth that's been simmering for hours, or bouncy and chewy long strands of cold udon with a deep brown soy- and dashi-based dipping sauce.

Top your udon with spring onions (scallions), grated ginger, tenkasu (crunchy bits of fried tempura batter) or whatever your heart desires, grab a small paper cup of water and take your tray to the tall tables, standing wherever you can fit. Have a big slurp of the dashi and enjoy.

Kake udon　かけうどん
The most basic of them all, but there really is beauty in simplicity: thick, chewy strands of udon in a warm, savoury broth. The delicate, smoky flavours from the katsuobushi (dried bonito flakes) and kombu (dried kelp) are best enjoyed with just a light scattering of green onions on top and tenkasu for texture. A firm favourite, and really the best way to tell how good an udon shop is.

Tempura udon　天ぷらうどん
This is what you order when you're looking for fun, excitement, a good (and very filling) time for lunch. I can't think of a much better pairing than big chunky udon and crispy, crunchy fried vegetables and prawns (shrimp). For the first bite, it's got to be the tempura alone, then dip it into the broth and enjoy the flavour of them together. What a treat.

Niku udon 肉うどん
One of my favourites: beef and onions are slowly simmered until meltingly tender and the onions disintegrate at just a touch. Soy sauce, mirin and sake meld with the light dashi, and the unctuous fat from the meat comes out into the broth making it slightly richer. Very often, you can top with benishoga (pickled ginger) to add a welcome brightness and zing to the dish, or top with a scattering of shichimi togarashi for a citrussy spice-led bite.

Chikara udon 力うどん
This one is more of a winter dish. I have strong memories of eating this in midwinter and feeling like all my problems were solved. It's exactly what's needed when there's an icy chill in the air. Udon is served in dashi broth, topped with a double portion of grilled kirimochi (cakes made from glutinous rice; see page 18) with a good bit of char and crunch on the outside while the insides are super stretchy. Spring onions (scallions) top the whole thing and you have yourself the most warming, comforting lunch.

Kare udon カレーうどん
The obsession with Japanese curry continues from breads to lunch sets and now udon. The mild sauce is mixed with savoury dashi broth to create a creamy, thick sauce that encases each noodle. The top tip, if you really know what's up, is to get a dab of salted butter on top, or a side of karaage (fried chicken; see page 149) for the ultimate lunch experience. What could beat curry, noodles and fried chicken?

Kitsune udon きつねうどん
I don't think there is anything much more comforting than a thick fried tofu pocket that has been simmered in a sweet and savoury sauce until it turns a beautiful and luscious dark brown. It forms a delicious blanket atop the bowl of noodles.

Tanuki udon たぬきうどん
This is a kind of introductory-level tempura udon – the one to go for if you're not looking for the full big-bang experience. I mean, it's lunch after all, so maybe you're not up for having a big nap afterwards. This one is made with tenkasu, what you could call the byproduct of tempura – crunchy little sprinkles of fried batter that add a welcome crunch on top of your noodles. Part of the fun is that it turns soggy as you're eating, which is equally as delicious and just enables you to have a meal with several textures.

Wakame udon わかめうどん
For an umami punch, you can't go wrong with wakame (a type of dried seaweed; see page 23) udon – probably the most slurpable udon of the lot. It's savoury, light fare for lunch with silky strands of seaweed on top. The high glutamate content from the seaweed creates an even richer and deeper flavour in the already savoury dashi broth.

family favourites

みんなの大好物

This chapter is all about comfort and joy: these are the dishes you'll crave when you come home from a long day at work, or turn to when you're cooking something for someone you love. They're the kind of recipes you'd find at a local Japanese eatery, the sort of place run by just one woman, working singlehandedly on the pans and front of house, who's been making and perfecting her dishes over a lifetime.

Many of the recipes in this chapter are ones that I've grown up with and have a deep connection to. Things like Nikomi Hamburg (stewed burgers; see page 88), Nikujaga (meat and potato stew; see page 104) or Soborodon (ground chicken and egg rice bowl; see page 103) remind me of my mum. Others are recipes that I cooked when I first moved to Japan, for people I cared about and who made me feel like family, such as Kaki Furai (fried oysters; see page 114), Yasai Korokke (vegetable croquettes; see page 109) and Harumaki (Japanese spring rolls; see page 115). Some are simple, while others require a little more effort. I understand that deep-frying may feel intimidating, but it can actually be quite time-efficient (as long as you clean up as you cook).

beef and onion rice bowl

gyuudon

Serves 2

2 tbsp soy sauce

1½ tbsp sake

1½ tbsp sugar

1 tbsp mirin

½ white onion, finely sliced

200g (7oz) beef, finely sliced

To serve

2 tsp vegetable oil

2 eggs

2 servings of steamed rice (see page 30)

1 tbsp benishoga (pickled ginger) (optional)

A comforting bowlful that is a surefire remedy for a late night out. Making it at home is the best, but if you've ever been to Japan and eaten at the chain called Sukiya, this is essentially the glorified version. My rendition has a more flavourful punch and a nice kick from the benishoga (pickled ginger). It's not traditional, but I love adding a fried egg at the end to give some creaminess to the whole dish.

A note on the beef: there's no need to use wagyu or anything super fancy, but do choose a cut with a higher fat percentage or that has fat running through it. You want the meat to melt in your mouth, not be chewy.

Put 200ml (7fl oz/scant 1 cup) water, soy sauce, sake, sugar and mirin in a lidded pan over a medium heat and bring to a simmer. Simmer for 5 minutes, then add the onion and cook until the onion has softened (about 5 minutes).

When the onion is soft, reduce the heat to low, then add the beef and stir so it cooks evenly (2–3 minutes). Skim off any scum that comes to the surface with a slotted spoon. Once the meat and onions are cooked, place the lid on the pan and turn off the heat.

When you're ready to eat, heat the oil in a frying pan (skillet). When hot, crack in the eggs and fry for 3–4 minutes so that the underside is crispy and the yolk is still soft.

Divide the meat between two bowls of steamed rice, drizzle over a couple of tablespoons of sauce and top each with a fried egg. Serve the benishoga on the side, if you like.

FAMILY FAVOURITES 81

FAMILY FAVOURITES

Japanese beef hotpot

sukiyaki

Serves 4

80g (2¾oz) shirataki noodles

1 tsp neutral oil, such as rapeseed (canola) or sunflower

1 leek, sliced diagonally lengthways into 2cm (¾in) chunks

50g (1¾oz) shiitake mushrooms

150g (5½oz) tofu, cut into 1.5cm (⅝in) slices

200g (7oz) beef, finely sliced

For the broth

3½ tbsp mirin

3½ tbsp soy sauce

4 tsp sugar

To serve

4 egg yolks, in separate small bowls

steamed rice (see page 30)

I hadn't had proper sukiyaki until quite recently. I think there are two schools of thought when it comes to Japanese hotpot dishes: the shabu-shabu types and the sukiyaki types. I always thought I was a shabu-shabu person, as it feels so luxurious to go out to a restaurant and be served beautifully poached meat and vegetables. But having a taste of proper sukiyaki changed me. It's a more deeply flavoured dish that's served with raw egg yolk as a dipping sauce. It's a special-occasion dish, yet it's deceptively simple to make.

The shirataki noodles are essential here. Made from the underground corms of the konjac plant, they have an almost translucent appearance and absorb the flavours of whatever they are cooked with. Shirataki are available from Asian supermarkets and many Western supermarkets, where they are sometimes sold as Miracle Noodles, because they have almost no calories.

For the broth, combine the mirin, soy sauce, sugar and 2 tablespoons of water in a saucepan, bring to the boil then reduce the heat and simmer for 2 minutes. Pour into a heatproof measuring jug and set aside.

In the same pan, bring 500ml (17fl oz/2 cups plus 2 tablespooons) water to the boil, add the shirataki noodles and boil for 3 minutes. Drain, then set aside.

Heat the oil in the same pan, add the leek and cook for 2–3 minutes, stirring, until browned all over. Add one-third of the broth to the pan, then add the shiitake mushrooms, cooked shirataki noodles and tofu. Let this simmer for 3–5 minutes over a medium heat until everything starts to soften and reduce.

When the broth in the pan starts to reduce, add 2 tablespoons more broth and cook for a couple of minutes until it reduces again; repeat twice more until there is around 3 tablespoons of broth remaining.

Add the sliced beef to the pan and cook for 2 minutes just until the pinkness goes. Serve the pan to the table for people to help themselves with the egg yolks in separate bowls for dipping the meat into. Serve with steamed rice.

Note: People with compromised immune systems are advised to avoid raw eggs.

FAMILY FAVOURITES

katsu curry

katsu kare

Serves 4

VO

For the curry

1 tbsp neutral oil, such as rapeseed (canola) or sunflower

2 onions, very finely sliced

1 tsp garam masala

½ tsp chilli flakes

3 potatoes, cut into sixths

2 carrots, cut on an angle to make 6–7 even chunks

4 curry cubes (around 75g/2½oz)

1 tbsp ketchup

1 tbsp okonomiyaki sauce (use a vegan one, if necessary; see page 22)

1 tbsp butter

100g (3½oz) shimeji or chestnut mushrooms

For the katsu

4 pork chops (500g/1lb 2oz total weight)

50g (6 tbsp/1¾oz) plain (all-purpose) flour

1 egg, whisked

100g (3½oz) panko breadcrumbs

300ml (10½fl oz/1¼ cups plus 1 tbsp) neutral oil, such as rapeseed (canola) or sunflower

salt

To serve

steamed rice (see page 30)

rakkyo or fujinzuke pickles

I couldn't write a book on Japanese home cooking without including a curry, and it had to be the most popular – katsu curry, made with breaded, fried pork cutlet. This is the easiest version, made using curry cubes. These are what everyone in Japan uses, as every cook will have a couple of packs in their pantry ready for a speedy meal. I always add a few extra ingredients to make the curry extra delicious and to suit my tastebuds more.

The katsu element is easier to make than you might think and it has a delicious crunch. Feel free to fry sliced aubergine (eggplant) for a vegetarian version. Common curry toppings, if you want to go the extra mile, are a fried egg, grated cheese and rakkyo (sweet vinegar-pickled Chinese onions) or fujinzuke pickles (pickled root vegetables with a sour, sweet and soy sauce flavour), both available at Asian supermarkets.

A cooking thermometer would be useful for this recipe.

For the curry, heat the tablespoon of oil in a large, lidded saucepan over a low-medium heat. Add the onions and cook slowly for 15 minutes, or until very soft and slightly caramelized. Add the garam masala and chilli flakes and cook for 5 minutes more. Add the potatoes, carrots and 500ml (17fl oz/2 cups plus 2 tablespoons) water. Cook over a low heat for 15–20 minutes, or until the potatoes are soft.

Add the curry cubes, ketchup, okonomiyaki sauce, butter and mushrooms. Let this simmer, stirring occasionally, for a further 10 minutes until the curry has thickened. Turn off the heat and cover with the lid to keep warm.

Meanwhile, for the katsu, bash the pork chops with a rolling pin to a thickness of 1.5cm (⅝in) and slice incisions in the fat at the top (this will prevent curling as it cooks). Season with a pinch of salt and set aside while you sort out the breading.

Put the flour in one bowl, the whisked egg in a separate bowl and the panko in a final bowl. Dip the pork pieces in the flour, shaking off any excess, then the egg and, finally, the panko. Set aside.

Heat the 300ml (10½fl oz/1¼ cups plus 1 tablespoon) oil in a large heavy-based pan, filling it no more than half-full. When it gets to 170°C (340°F), add the breaded pork pieces, two at a time. If you don't have a cooking thermometer, dip the tip of a wooden or bamboo chopstick into the oil. When it's hot enough, a steady stream of small air bubbles will rise to the surface. Fry for 3 minutes on one side, then flip with tongs and fry for 2 minutes on the other side.

Turn off the heat, return all the pork pieces to the hot oil and cook them in the residual heat for 3 minutes, or until completely cooked through. Transfer to a cooling rack set over a plate to drain the excess oil, then cut into thick slices.

Spoon the curry sauce over bowls of steamed rice and top with the sliced pork. Serve with pickles on the side.

FAMILY FAVOURITES 85

FAMILY FAVOURITES

curry udon

kare udon

Serves 2

VO

1 tsp neutral oil, such as rapeseed (canola) or sunflower, plus 1 tbsp extra

½ white onion, finely sliced

120g (4¼oz) pork or beef, finely sliced

550ml (19fl oz/scant 2½ cups) dashi

1 tbsp soy sauce

1 tbsp mirin

2 packs fresh udon (350g/12oz total weight)

2 curry cubes (35–40g/1¼–1½oz total weight)

2 eggs

2 spring onions (scallions), finely sliced

This ten-minute meal is a fridge-raid dinner that's handy to have up your sleeve. The curry cubes are what make the dish so incredibly easy. Feel free to swap out the meat for mushrooms or leave it out altogether. If you don't want to make the curry base from scratch, you could always use leftovers from a katsu curry (see page 84) and thin it down with dashi until it's a pourable consistency.

Heat the teaspoon of oil in a large saucepan over a low-medium heat. When hot, add the onion and sliced meat and cook, stirring, for 3–4 minutes, or until the meat is cooked through. Pour in the dashi, add the soy sauce and mirin, bring to a simmer and cook for 5 minutes.

Meanwhile, cook the udon following the package instructions (this should take around 3 minutes), then drain, rinse and set aside.

Add the curry cubes to the saucepan, stirring them in well until fully dissolved. Leave to simmer for 5 minutes until the sauce has thickened. Once the sauce is smooth, add the noodles and let them heat through and absorb some of the flavour.

Meanwhile, heat the tablespoon of oil in a frying pan (skillet). When nicely hot, crack in the eggs and cook to your liking.

To serve, divide the kare udon between bowls, top with the fried eggs and scatter over the spring onions.

stewed burgers

nikomi hamburg

Serves 4

For the sauce

1 tbsp butter

1 onion, finely diced

150ml (5fl oz/scant ⅔ cup) canned chopped tomatoes

3 tbsp ketchup

3 tbsp okonomiyaki sauce (see page 22)

1 tsp sugar

1 tsp soy sauce

200ml (7fl oz/scant 1 cup) vegetable stock

100g (3½oz) mixed mushrooms, such as oyster, shiitake and chestnut (cremini) (optional)

For the burgers

25g (1oz) panko breadcrumbs

100ml (3½fl oz/scant ½ cup) milk

250g (9oz) minced (ground) pork and beef mixture

1 tsp soy sauce

1 egg, beaten

1 tbsp vegetable oil

salt and freshly ground black pepper

To serve

steamed rice (see page 30)

Essentially a burger without the bun – but the patty is extremely juicy and filled with sweetness from the cooked onions. There are a few ways you'll see a hamburg on a Japanese menu, such as cooked on a hot stone plate with demi-glace sauce, or served with grated daikon and ponzu (see page 91) for the more 'light-and-fresh-fare' kind of person. This is my favourite version. It's stewed in a rich tomato sauce until the meat is tender enough to melt in your mouth.

This dish always reminds me of my mum. There's something about the smell of slowly stewed rich tomato sauce with the hamburg simmering in it that made me so excited for dinner, and made for great leftovers that would be a gourmet lunch the next day. This feeling of nostalgia and comfort was brought back to me when I first moved to Japan and frequented a local bento shop in Yokosuka run by one older lady who always had this on the menu and would always sneak in an extra karaage or croquette on the side for me.

For the sauce, heat the butter in a large saucepan, add the onion and cook gently until softened, 4–5 minutes. Remove and set aside half of the cooked onion in a bowl for the burger. Add the chopped tomatoes, ketchup, okonomiyaki sauce, sugar and soy sauce to the pan and cook for 10 minutes until reduced slightly, then add the vegetable stock, bring to a simmer and cook, stirring, for a further 10 minutes.

For the burgers, combine the panko and milk in a large bowl. Set aside for a few minutes to let the breadcrumbs absorb the milk.

Add the minced pork and beef mixture, soy sauce, egg and the reserved cooked onion to the panko mixture. Season with a pinch of salt and a few cracks of black pepper.

Shape the burger mixture into four even patties in your hands. To cook, heat the oil in a frying pan (skillet) over a medium-low heat. When hot, add the burgers and cook for 3–4 minutes on each side until golden brown.

Transfer the burgers to the pan with the tomato sauce and cook for 15 minutes until they are completely cooked through. If using the mushrooms in the sauce, add them at this point and cook for a further 5–7 minutes.

Serve the burgers and sauce spooned over steamed rice.

FAMILY FAVOURITES

chicken and tofu burgers

tori hamburg

Serves 4

For the burger

75g (2½oz) firm tofu

250g (9oz) chicken thigh mince (ground chicken thigh)

25g (1oz) panko breadcrumbs

1 tsp soy sauce

1 tsp sake

10g (¼oz) spring onion (scallion), very finely sliced

2 tsp vegetable oil, for frying

salt and freshly ground black pepper

For the dipping sauce

4cm (1½in) piece of daikon

3½ tbsp ponzu (see page 22), plus extra to serve

To serve

4 shiso leaves (a Japanese herb reminiscent of basil; optional)

steamed rice (see page 30)

A lighter take on a burger, using chicken and a bit of tofu to keep the patties bouncy and light. I love the thought of this burger with grated daikon oroshi and fresh, citrussy ponzu, a salad on a side and, of course, a steaming bowl of rice. It's a more spring-like counterpart to the stewed and comforting tomato base of the Nikomi Hamburg (see page 88). I've made this using up odds and ends of fridge veg, such as edamame, carrots and hijiki seaweed, which I'd recommend, but I would add a maximum of around 50g (1¾oz) if you do so, to make sure the burger sticks together.

About 30 minutes to 1 hour before cooking, drain the tofu: put it on a plate lined with paper towels and place a weight on top to gently press out the liquid. I normally use a pan with a tin of beans on top.

Once the tofu is drained, crumble it into a bowl and add the chicken mince, panko, soy sauce, sake and spring onion. Season with salt and pepper, and mix well with your hands. Once it's come together, form into four even patties.

Heat the oil in a frying pan (skillet) with a lid on medium heat. When hot, cook the burgers for 3 minutes on each side, then add 1 tablespoon of water, put the lid on the pan and cook for 5 minutes, or until completely cooked through.

To make the dipping sauce, finely grate the daikon (a Japanese grater is ideal here, see page 27) into a bowl. Squeeze out some of the water, then shape into four small mounds – one on each of four plates. Pour a drizzle of ponzu over each.

Serve the burgers with a shiso leaf on top (if using), the dipping sauce, some extra ponzu on the side, and steamed rice.

marinated fried chicken

tori nanban

Serves 4

For the tartare sauce

2 eggs, hard-boiled (hard-cooked)

4 tbsp mayonnaise

1 tbsp ketchup

1 spring onion (scallion), finely chopped

freshly ground black pepper

For the chicken

2 eggs

150g (5½oz) plain (all-purpose) flour, seasoned with a pinch of salt

400g (14oz) chicken thighs, chopped into roughly 5cm (2½in) cubes

200ml (7fl oz/scant 1 cup) neutral oil, such as rapeseed (canola) or sunflower

For the marinade

2 tbsp rice vinegar

1½ tbsp soy sauce

1½ tbsp sugar

½ garlic clove, finely grated

To serve

steamed rice (see page 30)

¼ head cabbage, finely sliced

This version of fried chicken is a lot easier than the classic izakaya dish Karaage (see page 149) and reaps the rewards. Although there are a few different elements, none are complicated – it might just require another bowl or two to be washed up. The chicken is fried, then marinated in a sweet and sour sauce, so don't expect super-crispy, double-fried chicken. That said, the fried batter is soaked with flavour, and it's all topped with a rich tartare sauce. This also makes a great sandwich filling, so I highly recommend leaving some for leftovers and stuffing it in white bread (crusts off for the most pleasurable eating experience) and adding some finely sliced cabbage.

Start by making the tartare sauce. Chop the eggs finely and put in a bowl along with the mayonnaise, ketchup and spring onion. Season with black pepper, then mix well and taste to check the seasoning. Set aside.

For the chicken, get out two bowls. Whisk the eggs in one and put the seasoned flour in the other. Coat the chicken pieces first in the flour, then the egg, then give them a light coating of flour again.

In a shallow pan, heat the oil over a medium-low heat. When it's hot, cook the chicken for 3–4 minutes on each side, making sure the pieces are evenly golden brown and cooked through. This should resemble shallow-frying, not deep-frying. It shouldn't take too long, as the chunks are small. Remove with a slotted spoon and transfer to a plate lined with paper towels to drain.

While the chicken is frying, mix the marinade ingredients in a bowl and stir until the sugar is completely dissolved. Dunk the chicken pieces in the marinade and serve on a warmed plate, with the tartare sauce on the side, with steamed rice and sliced cabbage.

FAMILY FAVOURITES 93

enoki mushrooms wrapped in pork belly

buta to enoki maki

Serves 2

200g (7oz) pack enoki mushrooms

12 slices (about 200g/7oz) thinly sliced frozen pork belly, defrosted

1 tbsp cornflour (cornstarch) or potato flour, for dusting

1 tbsp vegetable oil

salt and freshly ground black pepper

For the sauce

2 tbsp soy sauce

2 tbsp mirin

1 tbsp sugar

1 tbsp sake

1cm (½in) fresh root ginger, finely grated

To serve

1 tsp sesame seeds

steamed rice (see page 30)

miso soup (see page 31)

leafy salad of your choice

I made this dish time and time again when I first moved to Japan – it's easy and delicious. The texture of the enoki mushrooms really makes it; I'm afraid there's no substitute for them, but you can find enoki at any well-stocked Asian supermarket and some Western supermarkets. If you can't find them, for a different style of dish you could use green beans (which my mum used to do), asparagus spears or even kirimochi (see page 18). Serve the rolls with steamed rice, miso soup and a side salad if you're so inclined. It works equally well as a donburi or rice bowl – just layer a steaming bowl of rice with five or six rolls, adding an egg yolk to the middle so you can dip the rolls as you eat.

This recipe calls for very thinly sliced 'shabu-shabu'-style pork belly, which you can find in the frozen section of Asian supermarkets. If you can't get this, unsmoked streaky bacon is a good alternative.

Cut the tough root ends off the enoki and discard. Separate the enoki into 12 even-sized bunches.

Season the pork belly slices with salt and pepper and roll the slices around the enoki bunches to form 12 rolls. Lightly dust the rolls with the cornflour and set aside.

Heat the oil in a frying pan (skillet) over a medium heat. When hot, fry the rolls, turning until browned on all sides and the pork is fully cooked, about 6 minutes. This will need to be done in two batches.

Set the rolls aside on a plate and keep warm while you make the sauce in the same pan. Add the soy sauce, mirin, sugar, sake and ginger to the pan and heat through, scraping up any browned bits from the base of the pan. Cook, stirring, until the sugar has dissolved and the sauce has thickened.

Return the rolls to the pan and let the sauce coat them and get a bit sticky. Finally, sprinkle with sesame seeds and serve on a warmed platter with steamed rice, miso soup and salad.

mabo aubergine

mabo nasu

Serves 4

VO + VGO

1 tbsp neutral oil, such as rapeseed (canola) or sunflower, or more as needed

100g (3½oz) pork mince (ground pork)

4 small aubergines (eggplants), or 100g (3½oz) firm tofu, cut into cubes

1 garlic clove, finely grated

2cm (¾in) fresh root ginger, finely grated

½ negi or spring onion (scallion), finely sliced

1 tsp cornflour (cornstarch)

1 tsp toasted sesame oil

steamed rice (see page 30), to serve

For the sauce

1 tbsp brown miso

1½ tbsp doubanjiang

1 tsp soy sauce

1 tsp sugar

1 tsp powdered chicken stock or vegetable stock

This is a Japanified rendition of the Chinese dish mapo tofu, but the Japanese version is more savoury and salty, with a slightly thicker sauce. It's a strong contender for weekly dinner rotations, depending on what you have in your fridge. I love the combination of pork mince and aubergine (eggplant), but it works well with tofu – or make it vegetarian or vegan by omitting the meat and using tofu or vegan mince and substituting vegetable stock powder. It's a little spicy, very savoury and super saucy, so it's perfect to top steamed rice and eat with a big spoon.

Negi are a type of Japanese spring onion. If you can't find them, use spring onions (scallions) instead. Doubanjiang, also called fermented chilli bean paste or spicy bean paste, is a fiery, savoury paste made from fermented broad (fava) beans. You can find it in Asian supermarkets and in many Western supermarkets.

For the sauce, put the miso, doubanjiang, soy sauce, sugar and powdered stock in a bowl with 200ml (7fl oz/scant 1 cup) water, mix well and set aside.

Heat the oil in a frying pan (skillet) over a medium heat. Add the pork and cook, stirring, until browned and crispy and the fat has rendered out, about 5 minutes. Transfer the pork to a plate using a slotted spoon, leaving the oil behind in the pan. Add the aubergine and cook gently, turning until browned all over and meltingly tender, about 6–8 minutes. Add a touch more oil to the pan, if needed.

Return the pork to the pan and add the garlic and ginger. Stir gently so as not to break up the aubergines and cook for 2–3 minutes until fragrant. Stir the sauce mixture into the pan and let it simmer for 2–3 minutes, then add the negi and cook for a further 5 minutes until the sauce has reduced.

Mix the cornflour with 2 tablespoons of water and add to the pan, mixing gently. Let it simmer for 2–3 minutes until thickened, then stir in the sesame oil. Serve immediately alongside a pile of steamed rice.

FAMILY FAVOURITES

salmon grilled in foil

salmon no foil yaki

Serves 2

2 x 100g (4¼oz) salmon fillets

125g (4½oz) mixed mushrooms, sliced

1½ tbsp butter

2 tbsp soy sauce

pinch of salt and freshly ground black pepper

To serve

finely sliced spring onions (scallions)

micro herbs of your choice (optional)

otsukemono (pickled cucumbers) (optional)

steamed rice (see page 30)

This is an incredibly easy dinner that requires just a few ingredients. It's surprisingly theatrical: when you open up the cartouche-esque foil package, the steam wafts out, bringing the welcoming smell of buttery soy sauce. This would be the perfect dish for cooking over a live fire when you go camping, too.

My favourite mushrooms to use are enoki for texture and maitake (hen of the wood mushrooms) for their earthy flavour. Shiitake works well and provides a stronger flavour, and sliced chestnut (cremini) mushrooms would also be delicious.

Preheat the grill (broiler) to high (about 250°C/475°F).

Lay out two pieces of foil, about 30 x 25cm (12 x 10in). In the centre of each, lay out half of the mushrooms, then top with a salmon fillet, half of the butter and pour 1 tablespoon of soy sauce over each. Season with salt and pepper, wrap tightly and cook on the top shelf under the grill for 10–12 minutes.

Serve immediately with a scattering of spring onions and optional micro herbs, pickled cucumbers, if using, and a steaming bowl of rice.

To make most of that buttery soy sauce, I love having a second helping of rice, topping it with the sauce and mixing in a raw egg. It's my version of tamago kake gohan, a classic Japanese egg dish.

sweet and sour prawns

ebi chilli

Serves 2

For the sauce

2cm (¾in) fresh root ginger, finely grated

1 garlic clove, finely grated

2½ tbsp ketchup

½ tbsp toasted sesame oil

½ tbsp soy sauce

1 tsp sugar

For the prawns

1 tbsp neutral oil, such as rapeseed (canola) or sunflower

300g (10½oz) raw peeled prawns (shrimp)

½ negi or spring onion (scallion), finely sliced

1 tbsp cornflour (cornstarch) mixed with 4 tbsp water

To serve

steamed rice (see page 30)

furikake (see page 64)

This is a Chinese takeaway classic that's been Japanified and made more suitable for home cooking. There's no need to deep-fry the prawns (shrimp) – a simple pan-fry will do, and they're then coated in a lip-smacking sauce. This works with pork as well – just substitute pork loin or chop, sliced into thin pieces.

Don't discard the shells from the prawns. They work really well as a base for miso soup (see page 31) and they make a rich dashi stock. Negi are a type of Japanese spring onion. If you can't find them, use spring onions (scallions) instead.

First, make the sauce: combine the ginger, garlic, ketchup, sesame oil, soy sauce and sugar in a bowl and set aside.

For the prawns, heat the oil in a frying pan (skillet) over a medium-high heat and fry the prawns until mostly cooked, 2–3 minutes. The exterior of the prawns will be a light blush pink.

Add the sauce and the negi, reduce the heat to medium and let it simmer for 2–3 minutes, then add the cornflour mixture. Stir and let the sauce thicken, then serve immediately alongside steamed rice with a sprinkling of furikake.

FAMILY FAVOURITES

soborodon

ground chicken and egg rice bowl

Serves 2

For the chicken

1 tsp neutral oil, such as rapeseed (canola) or sunflower

200g (7oz) chicken thigh mince (ground chicken thigh)

2 tbsp garden (fresh) peas

1 tbsp soy sauce

1 tbsp sake

1 tbsp mirin

1 tbsp sugar

1cm (½in) fresh root ginger, finely grated

For the eggs

2 eggs

1 tbsp sugar

½ tbsp soy sauce

1 tbsp mirin

1 tbsp single (light) cream, or whole milk

To serve

steamed rice (see page 30)

1 sheet of nori, finely sliced

This is a dinner that I fondly remember my mum making me as a child. I would always sneak into the kitchen and have a bite of the eggs, which are deliciously sweet and savoury, while she was cooking – this ultimately meant we were left with a bit of an unbalanced final bowl rather than the usual 50/50 chicken-to-egg ratio. I guarantee every child – and adult – will love this dish.

I've used chicken for this, but pork also works well. You can also play around with the veg. I've always loved fresh garden peas, but you could also just omit completely and serve with some buttery peas or green beans on the side, or with a simple salad.

Heat the oil in a frying pan (skillet) over a medium-high heat. When hot, add the chicken and cook, stirring, until bits start to go brown and crispy and it's fully cooked through, 4–5 minutes.

Add the peas, soy sauce, sake, mirin, sugar and ginger to the pan, letting the liquid evaporate and be absorbed into the chicken. This should take around 2 minutes. Set aside.

In a bowl, whisk the eggs with the sugar, soy sauce, mirin and cream. Heat a small saucepan over a low heat, add the egg mixture and cook, stirring. You want to scramble these so they're fairly dry rather than having a super-soft, liquidy scramble.

To serve, spoon over two bowls of rice, with the chicken on one side and the egg mixture on the other, and the nori sprinkled on top.

nikujaga

meat and potato stew

Serves 4

1 tbsp neutral oil, such as rapeseed (canola) or sunflower

300g (10½oz) beefsteak, finely sliced

2 large potatoes (350g/12oz total weight), cut into 6 or so chunks

2 carrots (175g/6oz total weight), cut into 6 or so chunks

1 large white onion, cut into 8 wedges

150g (5½oz) shirataki noodles (optional)

½ tbsp hondashi (see page 16)

3 tbsp soy sauce

2 tbsp sake

1½ tbsp mirin

10g (¼oz) sugar

50g (1¾oz) green beans, trimmed

To serve

steamed rice (see page 30)

miso soup (see page 31)

dressed salad leaves

Just about every family has a recipe that's been passed down from their grandma or mum, and I think this is one of those dishes that reminds everyone of home. The name directly translates to niku ('meat') and jaga ('potato'). It really is exactly what it says: beef stewed with potato, carrot and onion. It's a humble dish with minimal ingredients and it really is the essence of Japanese home cooking. The dish is all about balance and making sure you have that sweet and savoury dashi flavour as it simmers away. It's even better the next day, so if you make it in advance, it will only soak up the flavours more.

Shirataki noodles have an almost translucent appearance and absorb the flavours of whatever they are cooked with. They are available from Asian supermarkets and some Western supermarkets, where they are sometimes sold as Miracle Noodles because they have so few calories. If you can't find them, just leave them out. You can also use beef mince for this, if beefsteak is hard to get hold of.

Heat the oil in a large lidded saucepan over a medium heat. When hot, add the beef and cook, stirring, for 2–3 minutes until golden brown. Add 350ml (12fl oz/1½ cups) water followed by the potatoes, carrots, onion and noodles, if using. Stir until everything is well incorporated, then add the hondashi, soy sauce, sake, mirin and sugar. Stir well, bring the mixture to the boil, then reduce the heat and simmer with the lid off for 20 minutes.

Add the green beans and simmer for a further 10 minutes. The broth should be reduced by more than half at this point and the potatoes tender; if not, keep simmering until the sauce is reduced to your liking.

This dish tastes better the longer it is left, as everything will soak up the flavours. Serve and enjoy with steamed rice, miso soup and some dressed salad leaves.

tempura rice bowl

tendon

Serves 4

V

For the tare

3 tbsp mirin

2 tbsp soy sauce

½ tsp hondashi or vegetarian alternative (see page 16)

1 tbsp sugar

For the tempura batter

1 egg, beaten

100g (3½oz) plain (all-purpose) flour, plus extra to dust (for the eggs)

For the vegetables and eggs

¼ kabocha squash, sliced into 1cm (½in) pieces; if unavailable use Japanese sweet potatoes (see page 210) or acorn squash

100g (3½oz) bunch of maitake (hen of the wood) mushrooms, or 4 fresh shiitake mushrooms

1 capsicum (bell pepper), cut into quarters

1 aubergine (eggplant), sliced into 2cm (¾in) rounds

2 onions, cut into sixths, secured with a toothpick

4 eggs, soft-boiled for 7 minutes, cooled in an ice bath, then peeled

300ml (10½fl oz/1¼ cups plus 1 tbsp) neutral oil, such as rapeseed (canola) or sunflower

steamed rice (see page 30), to serve

Serving tempura always makes a meal feel special. It really is a crowd pleaser (it's probably what I get requested to make the most at home) and it's versatile, too. It's easy to make it with all vegetables, or use prawns (shrimp) or tempura chicken to make it more hearty. The star of the show is the egg tempura, so I urge you to make this as part of the main event (pictured overleaf).

A tare is an essential part of Japanese cooking and can be used as a sauce, glaze, a broth for noodles (as in ramen) or for dipping. Here, the tare is the sauce that brings everything together. The whole point of this dish is that the rice should be lightly soaked with the savoury, slightly sweet and dashi-forward sauce and it should be drizzled over the tempura, too. It's up to you how much you want to pour on top, but I advise a light drizzle, and serving extra on the side to make sure you enjoy the crispy vegetables in all their glory.

A cooking thermometer would be useful for this recipe.

For the tare, mix all the ingredients with 3½ tablespoons of water in a small pan, bring to a simmer and cook for 3 minutes. Take off the heat and leave to cool. (The tare can be made in advance.)

For the batter, whisk 200ml (7fl oz/scant 1 cup) ice-cold water and the egg in a bowl, then sift in the flour, mixing until just incorporated. It's okay if there are a few lumps in it.

Prepare a frying station. Set a wire rack above a plate or metal tray to capture any excess oil. Have all the vegetables and eggs prepared on your far left, with the batter next to them, followed by the pan to fry everything and the draining rack next to that. This should allow you to have a smooth and mess-free process.

Heat the oil in a large, heavy-based pan filled no more than halfway to 175°C (350°F). If you don't have a thermometer, dip the tip of a wooden or bamboo chopstick into the oil. When it's hot enough, a steady stream of small air bubbles will rise to the surface. When the oil is ready, dip the vegetables into the batter using long chopsticks and then immediately add them to the hot oil to cook, one by one. They should take 2 minutes per side, but the kabocha may take longer as it's more dense. Ensure the oil remains at the correct temperature while you are cooking.

For the eggs, dust the exteriors with flour, then dip into the batter. Add to the hot oil and cook for 2 minutes, turning regularly so all sides are fried and the batter is crispy.

As each item is cooked, carefully remove it from the hot oil to the draining rack. Continue until all the vegetables and eggs are cooked. Halve the eggs just before serving.

To finish the dish, divide the rice among four serving bowls and top with a couple of tablespoons of the tare. Add a selection of vegetables and a halved egg each. Drizzle with another spoonful of tare and eat straight away.

FAMILY FAVOURITES

FAMILY FAVOURITES

FAMILY FAVOURITES

vegetable croquettes

yasai korokke

Serves 4

V

For the filling

500g (1lb 2oz) potatoes

500ml (17fl oz/2 cups plus 2 tbsp) neutral oil, such as rapeseed (canola) or sunflower for frying, plus 1 tbsp extra

1 carrot, cut into small dice

½ white onion, diced

100g (3½oz) sweetcorn (corn)

50g (1¾oz) petits pois or peas

2 tbsp butter

salt and freshly ground black pepper

For the dipping sauce

2 tbsp okonomiyaki sauce (see page 22)

2 tbsp ketchup

For the breading

1 egg

50g (1¾oz) plain (all-purpose) flour

75g (2½oz) panko breadcrumbs

The only thing better than having freshly fried food is the thought of having leftovers the next day. Korokke sandwiches are huge in Japan. There's something incredibly comforting about potato that's been deep-fried in breadcrumbs and then stuffed into slightly sweet white bread. I've stuck to vegetables that can be used fresh, frozen or canned to save a run to the supermarket. If you wanted to level it up, you could fry cubes of Spam and add them, too.

Peel and quarter the potatoes, then cook in a pan of boiling salted water for 15–20 minutes until tender. Drain, allow them to steam dry, then mash. The mash doesn't have to be completely smooth and creamy – it can have a bit of texture to it.

Heat the tablespoon of oil in a pan over medium heat, add the carrot and onion and cook, stirring, for 5 minutes until tender, then add to the mashed potato mix. Stir in the sweetcorn and peas, add the butter, season with salt and pepper and mix gently.

Shape the mash mixture into about 10 even-sized ovals and place on a plate. Chill in the fridge for 30 minutes to firm up.

Meanwhile, combine the sauce ingredients in a bowl and set aside.

When the croquettes are chilled, get the batter station ready: put the whisked egg in one bowl, the flour in another and the breadcrumbs in a third bowl. Dip the croquettes first in the in flour, then the egg and finally the panko.

To fry, heat the 500ml (17fl oz/2 cups plus 2 tbsp) oil in a heavy-based pan filled no more than halfway to 170°C (340°F). If you don't have a thermometer, dip the tip of a wooden or bamboo chopstick into the oil. When it's hot enough, a steady stream of small air bubbles will rise to the surface. When the oil is hot, carefully add 2–3 croquettes at a time so as not to overcrowd the pan. They should take around 2 minutes per side to cook until golden brown.

Remove the croquettes with a slotted spoon and transfer to a draining rack with a plate underneath to catch the drips, to drain any excess oil. Keep them warm while you cook the remaining croquettes.

Serve straight away with the sauce on the side.

Japanese savoury pancake

okonomiyaki

Serves 2

For the batter

¼ head of cabbage, finely shredded

1 negi or spring onion (scallion), finely sliced

100g (3½oz) nagaimo (Chinese mountain yam or cinnamon vine)

2 eggs, whisked

1 tsp hondashi or vegetarian alternative (see page 16)

140g (5oz/1 cup plus 1 tbsp) plain (all-purpose) flour

handful of grated mozzarella cheese (optional)

1 tbsp vegetable oil

For the filling

4 slices thinly sliced pork belly or unsmoked streaky bacon per pancake, or use prawns (shrimp) and squid for a meat-free alternative

1 kirimochi (see page 18) per pancake, sliced into small chunks

2 tbsp tenkasu (see page 53; optional)

Toppings

okonomiyaki sauce (see page 22) (if you don't have this, mix equal parts Japanese tonkatsu sauce with ketchup)

mayonnaise

your choice of: aonori seaweed, katsuobushi (dried smoked bonito flakes), benishoga (pickled ginger)

Okonomiyaki – a Japanese savoury pancake topped with a variety of savoury morsels and sauces – is hugely popular throughout the country. There are two main regional variations: the Osaka-style one is made with cabbage and nagaimo (mountain yam) in the batter to provide a fluffy pancake, while the Hiroshima-style one is a thin crêpe layered with a fried egg and filled with fried noodles. My favourite style is the former, which is found across the Kanto region and is what I grew up eating at home.

Traditionally, this would be topped with okonomiyaki sauce (see page 22), mayonnaise, aonori seaweed (see page 23) and katsuobushi (dried smoked bonito flakes) with benishoga (pickled ginger) on the side. I love lashings of sauce and go generous with the katsuobushi, which provides a really nice smoky flavour. The aonori adds an element of umami to the dish that you can only get from seaweed. You could, of course, go with just the sauce and mayonnaise if the other ingredients are hard to find.

The grated nagaimo is what gives this dish its light, fluffy texture, so it's worth tracking down. It's available from Asian supermarkets and is sometimes sold as Chinese mountain yam or cinnamon vine. Negi are a type of Japanese spring onion. If you can't find them, use spring onions (scallions) instead. Tenkasu are bits of fried tempura batter that add crunch (see page 53).

For the pancake batter, combine the cabbage and negi in a bowl. Grate the yam in a separate bowl – a Japanese grater (see page 27) is useful for this, or use the finest setting on a box grater. Mix in the eggs, hondashi and 150ml (5fl oz/scant ⅔ cup) water, then add the flour, mixing gently to form a batter. Add the cheese, if using, then mix the cabbage and negi through the batter and you're ready to fry.

Heat half of the oil in a large frying pan (skillet) over a medium-low heat. When hot, add the batter and spread it out. Top with pork slices/bacon, nestle in the kirimochi and tenkasu (if using) and allow to cook on one side. After 2–3 minutes, you need to flip the pancake – use a spatula to slide the pancake onto a plate, cooked side-down, cover with the pan and turn the whole thing over so that the cooked side is now facing up. Cook for a further 3–4 minutes.

Serve immediately, topped with okonomiyaki sauce, mayonnaise and your choice of aonori, katsuobushi or benishoga.

FAMILY FAVOURITES

111

mixed mushroom rice

kinoko takikomi gohan

Serves 4, with leftovers

V + VG

285g (1½ cups) short-grain rice

1 tsp neutral oil

50g (1¾oz) shiitake mushrooms, trimmed and sliced

50g (1¾oz) enoki mushrooms, trimmed and separated

50g (1¾oz) maitake mushrooms (hen of the wood mushrooms), trimmed and sliced (optional)

2 garlic cloves, finely sliced

2½ tbsp soy sauce

2 tbsp sake

2 tbsp mirin

1 tsp sugar

1 tsp hondashi or vegan alternative (see page 16)

2 tsp toasted sesame oil (optional)

1 tsp toasted sesame seeds

To serve

freshly ground black pepper (optional)

1 tbsp butter (optional)

This comforting recipe, filled with earthy flavours, is one for all the mushroom lovers out there – a satisfying one-pot dish filled with so many edible jewels. It is often made in a rice cooker, but I've used a lidded casserole (Dutch oven) on multiple occasions and find it works just as well (and is actually a lot quicker).

   I love putting my twist on this by adding a dab of butter and black pepper when serving, which really makes it well rounded and delicious. If you prefer, I'd suggest adding a tablespoon of toasted sesame oil to the rice before cooking. If you can't find maitake mushrooms, just increase the amount of shiitake and enoki to 75g (2½oz) each.

Put the rice in a sieve (strainer), rinse well under cold running water until the water runs clear, then drain. Transfer to a heavy cast-iron or non-stick pan with 400ml (14fl oz/1¾ cups) water and set aside to soak for 30 minutes.

   Meanwhile, heat the oil in a large frying pan (skillet) over a medium heat. When hot, add the mushrooms in one layer. Let them sit for 2–3 minutes, without stirring, until browned on the bottom, then mix gently and brown on the other side. Add the garlic at this point and cook for 2 minutes.

   Once the rice has soaked, add the soy sauce, sake, mirin, sugar and hondashi (and the sesame oil, if using) to the rice and stir gently to incorporate.

   Add the cooked mushrooms but do not mix! Let them sit on top of the rice, as this will ensure the rice cooks properly. Sprinkle the sesame seeds on top of the mushrooms, put the lid on the pan and, once you hear the water come to the boil, reduce the heat to the lowest level and cook for 14 minutes.

   Turn the heat off and keep the lid on for a further 10–15 minutes. Once the rice is done, gently mix it with a rice paddle or wooden spoon. Add a dab of salted butter and a few cracks of black pepper, if you like, and serve.

kaki furai

fried oysters

Serves 2

For the oysters

12 raw oysters, freshly shucked

500ml (17fl oz/2 cups plus 2 tbsp) cool water with the juice of ½ lemon squeezed in

50g (1¾oz) plain (all-purpose) flour seasoned with ½ tsp salt

1 egg, whisked

100g (3½oz) panko breadcrumbs

300ml (10½fl oz/1¼ cups plus 1 tbsp) neutral oil, such as rapeseed (canola) or sunflower

For the tartare sauce

2 hard-boiled (hard-cooked) eggs

1 tsp capers, rinsed and dried

5 cornichons

15g (½oz) parsley

4 tbsp mayonnaise

zest of ¼ lemon

salt and freshly ground black pepper

This was one of the first dishes I cooked for myself when I moved to Japan. I was home alone and decided to really cook up a feast. There's no need to fear deep-frying, especially when it's something as quick as this dish (so your kitchen won't smell for hours after). The oysters need only 2–3 minutes' frying, just until the breadcrumbs go brown. They will still be delightfully juicy and plump on the inside. I make a quick tartare sauce, but it's great with just okonomiyaki sauce (see page 22) or some Kewpie mayonnaise if you want to keep things simple.

A cooking thermometer would be useful for this recipe.

Prepare the oysters by soaking them in the lemon water mixture for 15–20 minutes, then draining.

While they're soaking, prepare your sauce. Chop the eggs, capers, cornichons and parsley and put in a bowl with the mayonnaise and lemon zest. Add a pinch of salt and pepper and set aside.

For the oysters, put the seasoned flour, egg and breadcrumbs in three separate bowls, so you have a breading station. Pat the oysters dry with paper towels, then lightly coat them in flour, dip in the egg and then into the breadcrumbs.

To fry, heat the oil in a large, heavy-based pan filled no more than halfway and let it come to 170°C (340°F). If you don't have a thermometer, dip the tip of a wooden or bamboo chopstick into the oil. When it's hot enough, a steady stream of small air bubbles will rise to the surface. Carefully place the oysters in the hot oil, working in batches as needed and making sure not to overcrowd the pan. Cook for 2 minutes on each side until golden brown.

When they're ready, remove the oysters with a slotted spoon, drain on a plate lined with paper towels and keep warm. Serve on a large warmed platter with the tartare sauce on the side.

Japanese spring rolls

harumaki

Makes 10 rolls

40g (1½oz) vermicelli noodles

150g (5½oz) pork mince (ground pork)

2 garlic cloves, finely grated

2.5cm (1in) piece of fresh root ginger, finely grated

40g (1½oz) shiitake mushrooms, stalks removed, sliced

½ large carrot, peeled and cut into long thin strips using a vegetable peeler

1 tsp vegetable stock powder

75g (2½oz) canned bamboo shoots, drained

45g (1^2/$_3$oz) Chinese chives, finely sliced (or use chives if unavailable)

10 spring roll sheets, about 22 x 22cm (8½ x 8½in)

400ml (14fl oz/1¾ cups) neutral oil, such as rapeseed (canola) or sunflower, for deep frying

sweet chilli jam, to serve

For the sauce

1 tbsp soy sauce

1 tbsp mirin

1 tbsp sake

1 tbsp toasted sesame oil

1 tbsp sugar

Harumaki are Japan's answer to spring rolls. They differ from the Chinese variety that tend to have more of a cabbage focus, and from the Thai summer rolls that use rice paper. In saying this, they're all hand-held morsels of joy. I stuff mine with pork, bamboo shoots, vermicelli noodles and a variety of vegetables, seasoning as the filling is made. Since everything inside is already cooked, it's just a matter of making sure the wrapper cooks to perfection, so it's crisp, light and flaky. I love serving these with sweet chilli jam or sriracha, but you could always use chilli oil or a mixture of soy sauce and vinegar.

A cooking thermometer would be useful for this recipe.

Put the vermicelli noodles in a heatproof bowl. Pour over boiling water from a kettle to cover and set aside for 10 minutes. Drain and set aside.

Combine the sauce ingredients in a small bowl and set aside.

Heat a frying pan (skillet) over a medium heat. When hot, add the pork and cook, stirring until slightly browned, 3–4 minutes. Add the garlic and ginger and cook, stirring, until fragrant.

Add the shiitake, carrot and vegetable stock powder, stir, cook for 2–3 minutes more, then add the bamboo shoots and chives.

Add the drained noodles to the pan along with the sauce in the bowl. Cook for 1–2 minutes until the sauce is incorporated, then remove from the heat and set aside to cool.

When the filling is cool, it's time to fill the wrappers and roll. Place a wrapper diagonally on a work surface, with a corner facing towards you. Put a tablespoon of filling in the lower half of the wrapper. Fold it over from the bottom, then roll upwards until only the top third of the wrapper is showing. Fold the two sides in towards the centre to enclose the filling, then roll upwards again. Brush the edges with water to seal. Set aside and continue until the wrappers and filling are used up.

To fry, heat the oil in a large, heavy-based pan filled no more than halfway and let it come to 170°C (340°F). If you don't have a thermometer, dip the tip of a wooden or bamboo chopstick into the oil. When it's hot enough, a steady stream of small air bubbles will rise to the surface. When the oil is ready, carefully add the harumaki in batches, being careful not to overcrowd the pan. Cook for about 2 minutes on each side, using chopsticks to turn, or until they are golden brown all over. Remove with the chopsticks and drain on a wire rack with a plate underneath to catch any oil.

Cut each roll in half and serve straight away with sweet chilli jam or a dip of your choice.

FAMILY FAVOURITES

FAMILY FAVOURITES　　　117

egg omelette rice

omurice

Serves 2

For the rice

1 tbsp neutral oil, such as rapeseed (canola) or sunflower

50g (1¾oz) chicken thigh or breast, cut into equal slices

½ onion, finely chopped

50g (1¾oz) of chestnut (cremini) mushrooms, sliced

½ red capsicum (bell pepper), sliced,

300g (10½oz) cooked rice (day-old preferable; see note, below)

4 tbsp ketchup, plus extra to serve

1 tsp salt

1 tsp sugar

a few cracks of black pepper

For the egg topping

4 eggs

1 tbsp mayonnaise

2 tsp butter

Another Japanese childhood classic. You might be surprised at how many Japanese dishes actually use ketchup as a main ingredient, but it adds a really nice sweetness and tang. It's best to use day-old rice here; if it's too fresh it will just result in a mushy filling, and here you want the grains to be separated and all the ingredients to be scattered through. It's one of those fridge-raid dinners, so you can use bacon instead of chicken and if you don't like mushrooms, just leave them out.

For the egg topping, I like to make mine into folded eggs rather than a full-on omelette as they do in restaurants – mainly because it's a lot easier than trying to make an omelette that's perfectly wobbly in the middle and made into an oval shape to top the rice, but also because I like having big wispy strands of egg going through the dish.

Heat the oil in a frying pan (skillet) over a medium heat. When hot, add the chicken. Cook, stirring, for 4–5 minutes, or until mostly cooked, then add the onion, mushrooms and pepper and cook for a further 2 minutes.

Once the onions are translucent, add the rice and stir it around in the pan until all the grains are separated. Add the ketchup, salt, sugar and pepper and stir through for a further 2 minutes. Transfer half of the mixture to a bowl, then flip out onto a serving plate. Repeat to make a second plate. Set aside and keep warm while you make the egg topping.

Whisk the eggs with 1 tablespoon of water and the mayonnaise in a bowl.

Heat the butter in a frying pan (skillet) over a low heat, then add half of the egg mixture. Softly scramble them for 2 minutes, using a spatula to break up the curds, then let the egg set for a minute. Carefully set the omelette over one bowl of rice.

Repeat using the remaining egg mixture and serve while hot.

Note: To safely store leftover rice, spread freshly cooked rice out on a large plate or shallow pan to quickly cool. When cool, chill straight away, cover and use within 2 days (or freeze).

FAMILY FAVOURITES

cream stew

western-style cream stew

Serves 2

150g (5½oz) skinless and boneless chicken thighs

100g (3½oz) kabocha squash, or use butternut squash

100g (3½oz) potatoes (no need to peel)

1 tbsp neutral oil, such as rapeseed (canola) or sunflower

2 tbsp white wine

1 tbsp plain (all-purpose) flour

100ml (3½fl oz/scant ½ cup) soy milk

3½ tbsp single (light) cream

1 tsp vegetable stock powder

50g (1¾oz) spinach

2 tsp butter

steamed rice (see page 30), to serve

This is a winter warmer and super popular in any Japanese household. You can easily make it with cream stew blocks (similar to curry roux and available online or from Japanese supermarkets), which is what most people tend to do – but when it's a recipe that only takes 15 minutes, then it would feel silly not to do it from scratch. I use the microwave to cook the squash and potatoes for ease and speed, but of course you can just boil them and use the boiled water instead of the measured water in the recipe.

Another thing to note is that I use unsweetened soy milk here, since it's what I normally have on hand, but just use regular whole milk if not. I'd avoid almond or oat milk, as these tend to have a naturally sweet flavour that will make the dish taste a bit funky.

Cut the chicken, squash and potatoes into bite-sized pieces of around the same size. Microwave the kabocha at 160W for 2½ minutes, then set aside. Cook the potatoes in the same way and set aside.

Heat the oil in a large frying pan (skillet) over a medium heat, add the chicken pieces and cook for 3 minutes on one side. Turn and cook for a further 2 minutes on the other side, or until completely browned and cooked through.

Pour the wine into the pan and let it evaporate, then add the squash and potatoes. Sprinkle over the flour and gently stir to coat the vegetables and chicken. Add the milk, cream, 150ml (5fl oz/scant ⅔ cup) water and the stock powder. Leave to simmer for 10 minutes until nicely thickened and piping hot.

Two minutes before serving, add the spinach and let it wilt. Stir in the butter just before serving with steamed rice.

chicken-stuffed lotus root

torizume renkon

Serves 2 as a light meal

For the filling

2 tbsp neutral oil, such as rapeseed (canola) or sunflower

½ onion, finely chopped

200g (7oz) chicken thigh mince (ground chicken thigh)

small handful of parsley, finely chopped

1 tbsp soy sauce

1 tsp sugar

1 tbsp sesame seeds

300g (10½oz) lotus root, sliced into 1cm (½in) rounds

1 tbsp cornflour (cornstarch)

salt and freshly ground black pepper

For the sauce

2 tbsp soy sauce

2 tbsp sake

2 tbsp sugar

To serve

steamed rice (see page 30)

cooked vegetables of your choice

I love the crunch of lotus root and it's fairly easy to buy online if you can't find it in Asian supermarkets. It has a nice crispness even when it's cooked and the light sauce sets it off nicely. It's delicious served with steamed rice and vegetables on the side but feel free to get the ketchup out and eat it with that, if you prefer!

To make the filling, heat half of the oil in a large frying pan (skillet) over a medium heat. When hot, add the onion and cook, stirring, until lightly caramelized, 5-7 minutes. Add the chicken mince and give it a good stir. Add the parsley, soy sauce, sugar and sesame seeds and season with salt and pepper. Set the filling aside in a bowl, keeping the pan to hand.

Dust the lotus root slices with cornflour. I do this by putting them in a sealable food bag, then shaking the bag until well coated. Sandwich the chicken mixture between the coated lotus slices to make neat sandwiches. You should end up with about 10 sandwiches.

Heat the remaining oil in the frying pan over a medium-low heat. Add the lotus root sandwiches in a single layer (you may need to work in batches). Cook for 2–3 minutes per side, turning carefully with a spatula halfway through, until lightly browned on both sides.

Meanwhile, stir the sauce ingredients together in a bowl. When the lotus root sandwiches are cooked, pour the sauce into the pan and cook for 1–2 minutes more, until the sauce is reduced and clinging to the lotus root.

Serve with steamed rice and vegetables of your choice.

122   FAMILY FAVOURITES

meat-stuffed peppers

nikuzume peeman

Serves 2

For the peppers

150g (5½oz) pork mince (ground pork)

¼ white onion, finely diced

1 egg, beaten

3½ tbsp panko breadcrumbs

4 Japanese capsicums (bell peppers), sliced into 2–3cm (¾–1¼in) rings

2 tbsp cornflour (cornstarch), to dust

1 tbsp neutral oil, such as rapeseed (canola) or sunflower

salt and freshly ground black pepper

For the sauce

3 tbsp ketchup

1½ tbsp okonomiyaki sauce (see page 22)

½ tbsp soy sauce

½ tbsp sugar

To serve

steamed rice (see page 30)

benishoga (pickled ginger)

sesame seeds

Japanese-style stuffed peppers are something I actively crave. For this recipe, I'm using a Japanese pepper variety that differs from the large capsicums (bell peppers) found in most supermarkets. They're bite-sized; a lot smaller and crunchier with a thinner skin and, when cooked, they're crunchy on the outside but juicy on the inside. I'd also argue that they don't have a super-strong flavour, so it's nice to serve them with a sauce to enjoy alongside. Any well-stocked Asian supermarket should have them, but if you can't get hold of them, sweet baby peppers make a good substitute.

Put the pork, onion, egg and panko breadcrumbs in a bowl, season with salt and pepper, mix well and set aside.

Dust the sliced peppers with cornflour. I do this by putting them in a sealable food bag, then shaking the bag until the peppers are well coated. Put the dusted peppers on a plate and stuff with the meat mixture.

Heat the oil in a large frying pan (skillet) with a lid over a medium heat. When hot, add the peppers in a single layer; you might have to do this in two batches. Cook for 2–3 minutes until browned on the bottom, then carefully flip them over and cook for a further 2 minutes. Pour in 100ml (3½fl oz/scant ½ cup) water, put the lid on and cook for 3–4 minutes, or until all the water has been absorbed or evaporated. Use a spatula to carefully transfer the stuffed peppers to a plate. Keep them warm while you make the sauce using the same pan.

Put all the sauce ingredients and 100ml (3½fl oz/scant ½ cup) water in the pan and cook, stirring, for 2–3 minutes, or until the sugar has dissolved and the sauce has reduced slightly.

Serve the peppers with the sauce drizzled over, with steamed rice, pickled ginger and sesame seeds sprinkled on top.

FAMILY FAVOURITES

'anything goes' nabe

nandemo nabe

Serves 2

VO + VGO

For the dashi

10g (¼oz) kombu (dried kelp; see page 23)

10g (¼oz) katsuobushi (dried, smoked bonito flakes)

For the goma dare sesame sauce

2 tbsp tahini

1½ tbsp sugar

1 tbsp mirin

1 tbsp soy sauce

1 tbsp rice vinegar

a drizzle of toasted sesame oil

For the nabe (hotpot)

1 tbsp soy sauce

1 tsp sugar

50g (1¾oz) Hakusai cabbage, or use sweetheart cabbage

50g (1¾oz) leeks, sliced on a diagonal into 2cm (¾in) pieces

30g (1oz) fresh shiitake mushrooms

50g (1¾oz) fresh shimeji mushrooms (optional)

150g (5½oz) soft tofu, cut into cubes

30g (1oz) nira (Chinese chives) (optional)

100g (3½oz) thinly sliced frozen 'shabu-shabu' pork belly, defrosted

To serve

steamed rice (see page 30)

ponzu (see page 22; optional)

crispy chilli oil (optional)

A nabe can be described as a Japanese hotpot, and this dish is essentially a light soup filled with vegetables. I've used my favourites, but anything you've got in the fridge is fair game, as is anything seasonal. To save time, you could use hondashi (see page 16), but if you have the time, do make the dashi from scratch. It's the star of the show. It's surprisingly easy to make and only takes ten minutes, rather than the hours you would put into a chicken stock.

The two dipping sauce suggestions are for ponzu (see page 22), which can be store-bought, and goma dare, a sesame-based sauce that's creamy and rich. I would normally serve it with both, but if you're feeling lazy, even just crispy chilli oil will do.

I use Hakusai, or Napa, cabbage as the base, as it's got a thick, watery stem, which allows the leaves to wilt in the broth but the centre to stay crunchy. Feel free to substitute with sweetheart cabbage in a pinch – you don't want anything too fibrous or it will take too long to cook. This recipe uses very thinly sliced 'shabu-shabu'-style pork belly, which you can find in the frozen section of Asian supermarkets. It is worth seeking out, as it adds a lot of flavour to the broth. If you can't find it or want to make the dish vegetarian or vegan, you can leave it out along with the katsuobushi.

Make the dashi first. Wipe the kombu clean using a damp paper towel, then put in a pan with 600ml (21fl oz/generous 2½ cups) water. Set aside to soak for 30 minutes.

After this time, put the pan over a medium heat and bring to a simmer. Let it simmer for 2–3 minutes; take the kelp out before the water boils. Add the katsuobushi and let it simmer over a low heat for 2 minutes, then turn the heat off. Strain the liquid through a fine-mesh sieve (strainer) and you have your dashi. Set this aside while you prepare the rest of the meal.

For the goma dare, mix all the ingredients with 1 tablespoon of water (you may need slightly more or less) in a bowl and set aside. Depending on the brand of tahini you use, the dip might be thinner or thicker, so adjust the amount of water to your liking. It should have a fairly thick but pourable consistency.

For the nabe, put the dashi in a large pan that has a lid, add the soy sauce and sugar and let it come to a simmer. Add the cabbage, leeks and shiitake mushrooms and let this simmer for 5 minutes. Once the shiitake have softened, add the shimeji mushrooms (if using), tofu, chives and pork belly. Leave to simmer over a low heat with the lid on for a further 5 minutes and the nabe is ready to serve.

Bring the pan to the table and ladle the nabe straight into bowls. Serve with side plates for the dipping sauce: one with goma dare and one with ponzu, and a big bowl of steamed rice. Once the nabe is served to everyone, either pour the ponzu over the whole soup or pick up the meat and vegetables and dip directly in the goma dare.

FAMILY FAVOURITES

FAMILY FAVOURITES

steak rice bowl

steak don

Serves 2

For the steak

250g (9oz) ribeye steak

1 tbsp neutral oil, such as rapeseed (canola) or sunflower, plus extra (optional)

salt and freshly ground black pepper

For the sauce

1 tbsp butter

2 garlic cloves, finely sliced

1½ tbsp soy sauce

1½ tbsp mirin

2 tbsp sake

To serve

steamed rice (see page 30)

2 egg yolks (or 2 eggs; optional)

This dish is a bit of a luxury, but who doesn't love a good steak? You can find amazing wagyu steak don in specialist restaurants, but people also make this at home for special-occasion meals, such as birthdays or Christmas. I find having a big ribeye to myself to be too heavy, so this dish for two is the solution. The beef is seared lightly, then cooked in a pan for a few minutes. It's then sliced and served on rice, topped with a simple butter soy sauce and an egg yolk. It's so delicious, and feels so special, yet uses just a few ingredients.

A cooking thermometer would be useful for this recipe.

Let the steak come to room temperature by taking it out of the fridge an hour before cooking. Season it generously with salt and pepper.

Heat the oil in a heavy-based pan over a high heat, add the steak and cook over a medium heat, searing it for 2 minutes and then turning it over and cooking for 2–3 minutes on the other side. I like my steak medium rare: when the steak gets to 55–60°C (131–140°F) internally, remove from the pan and set aside on a plate to rest. If you prefer a more well-done steak, leave it in the pan for a little longer.

While it's resting, make the sauce. Heat the butter in a pan. When foaming, add the garlic and cook, stirring, for about 2 minutes until fragrant (don't let it burn). Add the soy sauce, mirin and sake, stir well and cook for a further 2 minutes. Set aside.

Once rested, slice the beef as finely as you can.

Serve the steamed rice in bowls, topped with the sliced steak and a drizzle of the sauce, with an egg yolk in the middle to stir through. If you don't want them raw, you can fry the eggs in a bit of oil and serve them on top of the steak instead.

Note: People with compromised immune systems are advised to avoid raw eggs.

Okinawan taco rice

taco rice

Serves 2

For the spiced pork

1 tsp neutral oil, such as rapeseed (canola) or sunflower

200g (7oz) pork mince (ground pork); use one with a high fat content

½ onion, finely diced

75g (2½oz) fresh shimeji mushrooms, or chestnut (cremini) mushrooms, chopped

2 garlic cloves, finely chopped

2 tbsp ketchup

1 tbsp Worcestershire sauce

½ tsp soy sauce

½ tsp ground cumin

salt and freshly ground black pepper

For the toppings

50g (1¾oz) lettuce, finely sliced

100g (3½oz) cherry tomatoes, halved

40g (1½oz) mild cheddar cheese, grated

75ml (2½fl oz/⅓ cup) soured cream

To serve

steamed rice (see page 30)

Tabasco or other hot sauce (optional)

An incredibly moreish dish that hails from Okinawa, where US military troops have had a presence since the Second World War. It's inspired by the Americanized version of tacos, then Japanified – so it's gone through quite a few rounds of metamorphosis. Don't expect anything richly spiced or meat that's cooked for hours and falling off the bone; it's more like the Japanese version of Old El Paso taco seasoning mixed with pork and mushrooms, served on rice, with all the extra bits and bobs. It's really delicious, and such a good meal for a crowd – you can easily double or triple the recipe when you need to, and cook a big vat of rice.

Heat the oil in a pan over a medium heat. When hot, add the pork and the onion and cook, stirring, for 5 minutes until the fat has rendered out, the pork is starting to go brown and crisp at the edges and the onion has softened. Add the mushrooms and garlic and cook for a further 2 minutes, stirring.

Add the ketchup, Worcestershire sauce, soy sauce and cumin, then season with salt and pepper. Take off the heat and set aside. That's really all the cooking done.

Serve up a big mound of steamed rice and top it with the spiced pork, lettuce, tomatoes, cheese, a dollop of soured cream and a good few shakes of Tabasco or your favourite hot sauce, if you like.

FAMILY FAVOURITES

pork katsu rolls

buta maki

Serves 2 (makes 10 rolls)

3 umeboshi plums (see page 24), stones removed

10 slices thinly sliced frozen 'shabu-shabu' pork belly, defrosted

10 shiso leaves (optional)

300ml (10½fl oz/1¼ cups plus 1 tbsp) neutral oil, such as rapeseed (canola) or sunflower

finely sliced cabbage, to serve

tonkatsu sauce (I use Bulldog), to serve (optional)

For the breading

30g (1oz/3 tbsp plus 2 tsp) plain (all-purpose) flour

1 egg, beaten

75g (2½oz) panko breadcrumbs

I've spotted these several times recently in Japanese food magazines. Thinly sliced pork belly is rolled around a herby and tangy filling of shiso leaves (a Japanese herb reminiscent of basil) and umeboshi (salty, sweet pickled plums), before being breaded and deep-fried until crunchy. If you can't find shiso leaves, feel free to leave them out. If umeboshi are hard to find, you can use grated mozzarella for a different take on the dish.

The method is beyond simple and should come together in under thirty minutes. Of course, you can use this style of rolled katsu as inspiration for adding your own twist: putting some cheese in the middle, or perhaps wrapping vegetables and pork together – the world's your oyster.

This recipe calls for very thinly sliced 'shabu-shabu'-style pork belly, which you can find in the frozen section of Asian supermarkets. If you can't find the pork, you could use a rolling pin to flatten out a boneless skinless chicken breast as thinly as you can and use slices of it to wrap the filling.

A cooking thermometer would be useful for this recipe.

Mash the umeboshi plums to a paste in a bowl.

Lay out a pork belly slice on a work surface. Put a shiso leaf on the far right side and a teaspoon of umeboshi paste down the centre. Wrap the pork around the filling to fully enclose it, forming a long tube shape; set aside on a plate. Repeat with the remaining pork slices, shiso and umeboshi paste. You will end up with 10 rolls.

Get ready for the breading: put the flour in one shallow bowl, whisk the egg in another and put the breadcrumbs in a third shallow bowl. Dip the pork rolls first in the flour, then the egg and, finally, the breadcrumbs. Set aside on a plate.

To fry, heat the oil in a large, heavy-based pan filled no more than halfway and let it come to 170°C (340°F). If you don't have a thermometer, dip the tip of a wooden or bamboo chopstick into the oil. When it's hot enough, a steady stream of small air bubbles will rise to the surface. Add the breaded pork rolls, 3–4 at a time, making sure not to overcrowd the pan. Fry, using long chopsticks to turn them, for 4–5 minutes, until golden brown on all sides.

Remove and transfer to a plate lined with paper towels to soak up the oil; keep hot. Continue until all the rolls are cooked. Serve while still hot with the cabbage on the side and a bowl of tonkatsu sauce to dip the rolls, if you like.

the teishokuya 定食屋

The feeling of having a comforting meal at home at your family dining table is exactly what's encapsulated at a local *teishokuya*. Walking into a small hole-in-the-wall place like this, probably a ten-seater, between 11a.m. and 2p.m. will grant you a special kind of warmth in your soul. It's that feeling of having a really good home-cooked meal with love and care put into it. No frills, no pretentiousness, no reservations – it's exactly what you want. More often than not, it will be run by one woman – on the pans, on the tills, on the welcome. Somehow, someone who's over eighty has the energy to do all of this and make your lunch experience as perfect as can be.

There are a few star-studded classic recipes that you'll have to try, all served as a perfectly balanced meal of miso soup, a main, rice and pickles.

Hamburg ハンバーグ
A Japanese take on the Western hamburger, served – naturally – with rice. This meat patty is normally made from pork or a mix of pork and beef. It's incredibly juicy and made up with sweet onions and panko before being shaped and fried. Often it will be served on a cast-iron plate, still bubbling away as the juices ooze out and the rich demi-glace sauce coats it.

Karaage 唐揚げ
I mean, fried chicken – what can go wrong? Fried to perfection and crispy, it's a meal that you don't want to end. Marinated in a mix of soy sauce, ginger and garlic and fried in a light but crispy coating, it just needs a squeeze of lemon and to be eaten while it's still piping hot with a mound of steamed rice.

Kare rice カレーライス
Every *teishokuya* is going to have a different take on kare rice (curry rice). Some will have big chunks of potatoes, carrots and onion – a simple and effective trinity for a solid meal. You'll also find little shops where the beef has been stewing for hours over a low heat to create a rich, dark sauce with all the ingredients close to melting, served over a bowl of rice. Compulsory pickles are placed on the side, normally rakkyou, which are small shallots that are powerfully bright and vinegary. Especially at curry-focused lunch spots, you'll be able to add a range of toppings: tonkatsu (breaded deep-fried pork cutlet) is a solid choice, of course, as is a fried egg with the yolk oozing into the curry, or that kind of fake plastic cheese that's oh-so satisfying and nostalgic.

Sakana teishoku 魚定食
I guess this is the type of meal people immediately imagine when thinking of a Japanese lunch: a piece of grilled fish with 'all the trimmings'. Seems healthy and a safe bet, but when it's done right it really is the perfect lunch. Tender mackerel or salmon are the most popular types of fish you'll find, as they're filled with delicious oils to keep them tender, topped with a bit of grated daikon oroshi, citrussy ponzu and a big squeeze of lemon.

Shyogayaki 使用がやき
A simple pork stir-fry might easily be overlooked, but the punchy ginger and soy-based sauce served with it makes this dish so inviting. Thin slices of pork belly and sliced sweet white onions are stir-fried and simply served on a plate. Be sure to mop up every last bit of that sauce with the steaming mound of white rice.

Tempura 天ぷら
A bit of fish, a bit of veg, all deep-fried? Perfect! A light and crispy batter encases everything before you go one of two routes: dipping in salt for something seemingly sophisticated and light. Or you can go the mentsuyu route (see page 18): fill a bowl with the savoury and sweet sauce, stir in some grated daikon oroshi and grated ginger, and generously dip the tempura in until soaked. Eat with a big mouthful of rice; it's the only way to do it.

Tonkatsu トンカツ
Thickly sliced pork is tenderized, coated in flaky breadcrumbs that provide an audible crunch at the first bite, and deep-fried; it's always juicy and has the perfect ratio of fat and meat. Top with sauce (most likely Bulldog brand tonkatsu sauce will be on the table, but if you're lucky then you'll get the real-deal homemade version that's been slowly simmered) and a lick of mustard. Japanese mustard is much like English mustard – it's potent and immediately goes up your nose. Don't forget the shredded cabbage, kept in ice-cold water before serving, which provides crunch and freshness to your meal.

izakaya at home

お家で居酒屋

The *izakaya* is the heart of Japanese dining culture. The hustle and bustle of these traditional eating and drinking dens can be heard, smelled and even seen from far away. Small, smoke-filled alleyways will be filled with tiny shops, each with their own speciality dishes, whether it's yakitori (grilled chicken), oden (simmered vegetables and fish cakes in dashi) or kushikatsu (deep-fried vegetables and meats). In Japan, drinking and eating go hand in hand, and there are no ifs or buts.

Sharing dishes over good conversation is my favourite way of dining, and that's exactly what this chapter – in my opinion the most exciting one in the book – encapsulates. It's all about sharing and eating with good company. Although, in saying that, I've made many a night of eating in on my own while cooking a few of these recipes – putting some music on, having a drink and enjoying a relaxing evening to myself while reaping the edible rewards.

Japan has always had a 'sharing plates' concept, long before it became fashionable in restaurants the world over. Food has always been communal in Japan – this is ingrained in the culture. Going out for dinner is an activity that everybody loves. It's a way to celebrate friendship and form new bonds. Normally, you'll end up at a few *izakayas* per night, doing a little hop around a certain area and eating a few dishes at each.

This has made it tricky to work out how many people each recipe serves. It's not as easy as one dish per person, since you'll be having a bite of everything anyway. I would suggest making three to five dishes per two people, depending on what you choose. Obviously, making Karaage (fried chicken; see page 149), Buta no Kakuni (braised pork belly; see page 154) and Menchi Katsu (meat and cabbage croquettes; see page 146) to go with some beers would be quite a meat-heavy, beige feast (nothing wrong with that, though), but going for something like Tori Momo no Ponzu Sauce (chicken thighs with ponzu sauce; see page 173), Hotate to Ichigo no Carpaccio (scallop carpaccio with strawberries; see page 174) and Agedashi Nasu (dashi-marinated aubergines; see page 182) with a chilled glass of wine would be wonderful in the summer as a light dinner.

The point of this chapter is to surprise and delight. Some dishes, such as Potato Salada (the ultimate potato salad; see page 178), Gyoza (pan-fried dumplings; see pages 138–41) and Ham to Cheese no Katsu (ham and cheese katsu; see page 157), are absolute classics that you'll find on almost every *izakaya* menu, whether you're in Tokyo or Hiroshima. Others are more experimental, inspired by dishes I've eaten out that have taken me by surprise and that are now embedded in my mind. Still others are dishes that I've made at home on a whim and that have become firm favourites. Those latter dishes, in particular, are here to inspire.

Don't sweat the small stuff. Some of these dishes might be new to you, but if I'm able to multitask in the kitchen and make three of these at once, then trust me – you'll be able to as well. After all, cooking is about intuition: if you don't have strawberries for the scallop carpaccio, use grapes or blood oranges. If you don't like scallops, then use prawns (shrimp) instead. These recipes are merely guidelines that are designed to set you off on your own journey of exploration.

pan-fried dumplings

gyoza

Makes 50

200g (7oz) pork mince (ground pork) with a high fat content

150–200g (5½–7oz) cabbage, finely chopped

30g (1oz) nira (Chinese chives) or ordinary chives, finely sliced

65g (2¼oz) negi or spring onions (scallions), finely chopped

2 tbsp soy sauce

2 tbsp toasted sesame oil

1 tsp chicken or vegetable stock

1 tsp finely grated fresh root ginger

2 garlic cloves, finely grated

2 tbsp plain (all-purpose) flour

50 gyoza wrappers

2 tbsp neutral oil, such as rapeseed (canola) or sunflower, for frying

salt and freshly ground black pepper

To serve

soy sauce

malt vinegar

toasted sesame oil or chilli oil

steamed rice (see page 30; optional)

This is one of my favourite recipes, one that I come back to time and time again. Undoubtably the juiciest gyoza, and a great dinner option for when you have lots of people coming round. I keep these stocked in my freezer for an easy snack, but they're also great in nabe (Japanese stews or hotpots). Use a pork mince with a high fat content to keep the centres juicy.

You will find gyoza wrappers (also sold as gyoza dumpling wrappers or gyoza skins) in the freezer section of Japanese supermarkets. They are circular, made from wheat flour and are sold in packs of twenty-five or fifty. Be careful not to mistake them for wonton wrappers, which are square and made with egg, giving them a yellow hue.

Put the pork mince in a large bowl, add the cabbage, nira and negi, then add the soy sauce, sesame oil, stock, ginger and garlic, and season well with salt and pepper. Mix well until fully combined.

In a separate, small bowl, mix the flour with 2 tablespoons of water to form a sticky paste. This will be a 'glue' to seal the gyozas. Get ready to fill the wrappers, making sure to keep them covered with a clean dish towel as you work so they won't dry out.

Hold one wrapper in your left hand. Put a teaspoon of filling in the middle of the wrapper – don't overfill or it won't seal properly. Use a finger to evenly spread the flour and water 'glue' mixture all around the rim.

To enclose the filling and create the pleated folds, hold the dumpling in your left hand and fold it in half so it is semicircular in shape. Have your left index finger on the back of the wrapper and your left thumb on the front. With your right hand, place your index finger on the back of the front flap of the wrapper, near the top, and your thumb on the front outside of the wrapper. Use your right thumb to create the pleats, gently pressing down, starting at one end and working towards the other (you are aiming for 6–7 pleats). Secure each pleat with your left thumb while you form the rest. Make sure all the pleats are secured by pressing them with your thumbs and index fingers.

As you work, set the filled gyoza aside on a tray, making sure they have enough space between them to prevent them sticking together, and cover with a clean dish towel so they don't dry out. Repeat until all the wrappers and filling are used up.

At this point, if you're not going to cook and eat the gyoza right away, you can freeze them (see tip on page 141).

To cook the gyoza, heat 1 tablespoon of oil in a frying pan (skillet) with a tight-fitting lid over a medium heat. When the oil is hot, working in batches so you don't overcrowd the pan, place several gyoza in the pan, flat-side down, and cook for 1–2 minutes until the bases are browned (carefully lift one up and check the underside). When they are browned, add 2–3 tablespoons of water and cover the pan tightly with a lid. Let the gyoza steam for 2–3 minutes, or until thoroughly cooked through.

Serve the gyoza while still hot, with small bowls of your choice of dipping sauces: combine soy sauce, vinegar and sesame oil or chilli oil to your liking. Eat immediately with a mound of steamed rice, if you like.

Tip: To freeze the gyoza, place them on a tray in one layer and transfer to the freezer. Once frozen, put them in a sealable food bag. They can be stored in the freezer for up to 1 month. You can cook them from frozen: you'll just need to cook them on a slightly lower heat (low-medium) for a minute or two longer to let them thaw and for the bases to crisp up, then steam until the skins are translucent and the gyoza are cooked through.

crab cream croquettes

kani cream korokke

Makes 12 (serves 4 as a sharing plate)

300ml (10½fl oz/1¼ cups plus 1 tbsp) neutral oil, such as rapeseed (canola) or sunflower, plus 1 tbsp extra to cook the onion

50g (3½ tbsp) butter

1 medium white onion, diced

6 tbsp plain (all-purpose) flour

500ml (17fl oz/2 cups plus 2 tbsp) milk

200g (7oz) kanikama (imitation crab/crab sticks), torn

1 tsp sugar

1 tbsp soy sauce

1 tsp freshly ground black pepper

lemon wedges, to serve

For the breading

50g (1¾oz) plain (all-purpose) flour, seasoned with salt and freshly ground black pepper

1 egg, beaten

100g (3½oz) panko breadcrumbs

The absolute king of croquettes, with a creamy interior and a crispy, light exterior. I use imitation crab for ease, but feel free to use picked crab meat, if you prefer. I reckon a handful of chopped chives would be delicious if doing so. This recipe is a bit of a process, but it's so worth making on a weekend or to impress guests.

A cooking thermometer is useful for this recipe.

Heat the tablespoon of oil and the butter in a saucepan over a medium heat. When hot, add the onion and fry, stirring, until translucent, 5–6 minutes. Add the flour and whisk over the heat for 1–2 minutes until the whiteness is gone. Add the milk in three stages, whisking well between additions. Cook, stirring, for a further 2 minutes.

Add the imitation crab and cook, stirring all the while, until the mixture is thick and fairly solid, about 5 minutes more – if it is too soft it will be hard to shape later. Add the sugar, soy sauce and black pepper and taste to check the seasoning.

Whisk the mixture well and check the texture: it should be firm enough that it wouldn't fall from the pan if you upturned it. Transfer the mixture to a rectangular container, spread it over the base, cover and let it cool for 2–3 hours.

When cool, slice the croquette mixture into 12 equal pieces and roll into rounds using your hands. Set aside on a plate.

Next, set up your breading station: put the seasoned flour on a plate. Put the egg in a shallow bowl and the breadcrumbs on a separate plate. Dip the croquettes first in the flour, then the egg, then finally the breadcrumbs to give them a good coating. Set aside.

When you're ready to fry, heat the 300ml (10½fl oz/1¼ cups plus 1 tbsp) oil in a large heavy-based pan filled no more than halfway. When it gets to 170°C (340°F), add the croquettes in batches, taking care not to overcrowd the pan. If you don't have a thermometer, dip the tip of a wooden or bamboo chopstick into the oil. When it's hot enough, a steady stream of small air bubbles will rise to the surface. Cook the croquettes for 2 minutes on each side, using tongs to turn, until browned and cooked all the way through.

Gently lift from the oil and drain on a rack set over a plate to catch the drips. Keep warm while you continue cooking the remaining croquettes. Make sure the oil gets back to the correct temperature before cooking the next batch.

Serve hot with lemon wedges.

boiled dumplings

sui gyoza

Makes 25

100g (3½oz) spinach, blanched for 30 seconds and refreshed in cold water

200g (7oz) chicken thigh mince (ground chicken thigh)

1 large garlic clove, finely grated

1 tbsp toasted sesame oil

½ tsp sugar

25 gyoza wrappers

1 tbsp plain (all-purpose) flour

salt and freshly ground black pepper

To serve

chilli oil

soy sauce

This is a very simple, pared-back version of gyoza, made using chicken mince and spinach (pictured overleaf). I like these to have punch from garlic and plenty of black pepper, but you can adjust to your liking, adding more black pepper, or omitting it altogether. These are great served with soy sauce and lots of chilli oil for dipping. They're delicious on their own served with drinks, but you can also use them in soups for a more substantial meal.

You will find gyoza wrappers (also sold as gyoza dumpling wrappers or gyoza skins) in the freezer section of Japanese supermarkets. They are circular, made from wheat flour and are sold in packs of twenty-five or fifty. Be careful not to mistake them for wonton wrappers, which are square and made with egg, giving them a yellow hue.

Using your hands, squeeze as much water as you can from the spinach, then chop finely and put in a large bowl.

Add the chicken mince, garlic, sesame oil and sugar, and season with salt, adding black pepper to your liking. Mix with your hands until it forms a cohesive mixture.

In a separate, small bowl, mix the flour with a tablespoon of water to form a sticky paste. This will be a 'glue' to seal the gyozas. Get ready to fill the wrappers, making sure to keep them covered with a clean dish towel as you work so they won't dry out.

Place a teaspoon of filling the centre of a wrapper, then use a finger to spread the flour and water 'glue' all around the edges. Fold it into a half-moon shape and then overlap the two ends over each other, securing again with the glue. The finished dumplings should be the shape of tortellini (see overleaf).

As you work, set the filled gyoza aside on a plate, covering with a clean dish towel so they don't dry out. Repeat until all the wrappers and filling are used up.

To cook, bring a large pan of water to the boil. Working in batches, use a slotted spoon to gently lower the gyoza in. Boil them for 4–5 minutes until they float to the top and the skin starts to turn wrinkly, then remove with a slotted spoon, set aside on a plate and keep warm.

Serve immediately with small bowls of chilli oil and soy sauce for dipping.

IZAKAYA AT HOME 145

meat and cabbage croquettes

menchi katsu

Makes 15 (serves 6 as a sharing plate)

For the croquettes

250g (9oz) cabbage, sliced very finely (a food processor is useful here)

350g (12oz) minced (ground) pork (use one with a high fat content)

½ onion (100g/3½oz), finely chopped

2 tbsp Worcestershire sauce

10g (¼oz) panko breadcrumbs

25g (1oz) cornflour (cornstarch)

1 egg, beaten

salt and freshly ground black pepper

tonkatsu sauce (I use Bulldog), to serve

For the breading

50g (1¾oz) plain (all-purpose) flour

1 egg, beaten

150g (5½oz) panko breadcrumbs

350ml (12fl oz/2½ cups) neutral oil, such as rapeseed (canola) or sunflower

These crunchy croquettes are surprisingly light, even though the main ingredient is pork. Using minced (ground) pork with a high fat percentage keeps them super juicy when they're cooked. This is my version of a dish I first tried as an *omiyage* (a souvenir), given to me by a friend who was visiting the city of Tottori in western Japan. I've since continued to enjoy it at a couple of favourite local restaurants in Tokyo. These are delicious served hot and fresh, but if you have any leftover, put them in a sandwich the next day.

A cooking thermometer is useful for this recipe.

Put the sliced cabbage in a large bowl, add a large pinch of salt and massage it into the cabbage with your hands. Set the cabbage aside to soften for 15 minutes.

When the cabbage has softened, add the pork and the onion and mix with your hands so all the ingredients are well incorporated. Add the Worcestershire sauce, 10g (¼oz) breadcrumbs, cornflour and egg, season with salt and pepper and mix well with your hands.

Shape the mixture into 15 even-sized ovals and put on a plate in a single layer. Cover and chill them in the fridge for 1 hour to firm up.

Once they are chilled, get your breading station set up. Mix the flour, egg and 75ml (2½fl oz/⅓ cup) water in a bowl and whisk to form a smooth batter. Put the 150g (5½oz) breadcrumbs on a plate.

Dip each croquette in the batter, then coat generously in the breadcrumbs, getting as thick a coating as possible. Set aside and repeat until all the mixture is used up.

To fry, heat the oil in a large, heavy-based pan filled no more than halfway and let it come to 170°C (340°F). If you don't have a thermometer, dip the tip of a wooden or bamboo chopstick into the oil. When it's hot enough, a steady stream of small air bubbles will rise to the surface. When ready, carefully add 3–4 croquettes at a time, being careful not to overcrowd the pan.

Fry the croquettes for 7 minutes, or until cooked all the way through, flipping every couple of minutes using tongs. They should be a dark brown colour when done.

Once cooked, transfer to a draining rack with a plate underneath to catch the drips and leave for 5 minutes. They will continue to cook in the residual heat. Serve straight away with tonkatsu sauce.

IZAKAYA AT HOME 147

148 IZAKAYA AT HOME

Japanese fried chicken

karaage

Serves 4 as a sharing plate

500g (1lb 2oz) boneless chicken thighs

1 garlic clove, finely grated

1 tbsp finely grated fresh root ginger

3 tbsp sake

3 tbsp soy sauce

2 tbsp toasted sesame oil

1 tsp sugar

1 egg, beaten

400ml (14fl oz/1¾ cups) vegetable oil

2 tbsp plain (all-purpose) flour

2 tbsp potato starch

flaked salt

To serve

mayonnaise

lemon wedges

daikon oroshi (finely grated daikon radish; optional)

ponzu (see page 22; optional)

When I say this is the ultimate crowd pleaser, I mean it. Everyone that has tried this recipe loves it. The chicken is marinated, which keeps it so juicy and flavourful, and the batter is double-fried for a golden colour and a super-crisp texture. I've kept the serving suggestions simple – just mayonnaise and lemon wedges, which is how I prefer it – but it's also delicious with daikon oroshi (finely grated daikon radish) and a dash of citrussy ponzu (see page 22). If you manage to have any leftover, it's delicious stuffed into a sandwich with lots of finely sliced cabbage.

A cooking thermometer would be useful for this recipe.

Put the chicken thighs in a large bowl with the garlic, ginger, sake, soy sauce, toasted sesame oil and sugar and mix thoroughly. Cover and leave to marinate in the fridge for at least 30 minutes, or up to 6 hours, if time permits.

Thirty minutes before frying, add the beaten egg to the mixture, mix well and let it sit at room temperature while you heat the oil and get ready to fry.

Heat the oil in a large heavy-based pan filled no more than halfway and let it come to 160°C (320°F). If you don't have a thermometer, dip the tip of a wooden or bamboo chopstick into the oil. When it's hot enough, a steady stream of small air bubbles will rise to the surface.

While the oil is heating up, mix the flour and potato starch in a bowl. When the oil is ready, dust a few pieces of chicken in the flour mixture, then carefully add to the hot oil using a slotted spoon. Cook the chicken pieces for 2–3 minutes until lightly golden, then remove from the oil and transfer to a tray. Repeat this process until all the chicken is cooked, ensuring the oil remains at 160°C (320°F).

When all the pieces have had their initial fry, raise the oil temperature to 180°C (355°F) for the second fry. If you don't have a thermometer, just crank the heat up slightly – it should bubble aggressively once you drop the piece of karaage back in. When the oil is hot, return the chicken to the oil, cooking in batches as before, for a further 1 minute until golden.

Remove using a slotted spoon and sprinkle with flaked salt while still hot. Carry on until all the pieces have had their second fry. Serve hot with mayonnaise and lemon wedges, or with daikon oroshi and ponzu, if you like.

chicken meatballs

tsukune

Makes 30 (serves 4 as a sharing plate)

200g (7oz) chicken thigh mince (ground chicken thigh)

1 tsp salt

1 tsp potato starch

1 spring onion (scallion), finely chopped

1cm (½in) piece of fresh root ginger, finely grated

1 large garlic clove, finely grated

1 tbsp neutral oil, such as rapeseed (canola) or sunflower

1 tbsp soy sauce

1½ tbsp mirin

1 egg yolk, to serve

Yakitori (chicken skewers) is one of my favourite things to eat in Japan, without a doubt. There's nothing more tempting than walking past an alleyway filled with the smoky scent of chicken being cooked to perfection on a *hibachi* grill. It is hard to recreate this in a domestic kitchen, so I've created a more at-home, finger-food-style yakitori dish.

Tsukune are chicken meatballs that are made with mainly the thigh meat – with some cartilage added to provide a mix of texture. As cartilage is slightly harder to get outside of Japan, I've kept it to just the thigh mince here. The sauce is a lighter version of the long-cooked, sweet and sticky sauce you'd be served at a yakitori restaurant, and I serve it with a raw egg yolk for dipping, which adds a creamy component.

Put the chicken mince, salt, potato starch, spring onion, ginger and garlic in a bowl and mix well. Divide into 30 even-sized balls and put on a plate. Cover and chill them in fridge for 30 minutes to firm up.

Heat the oil in a large frying pan (skillet) pan and fry the tsukune in 2–3 batches, being careful not to overcrowd the pan. Fry the tsukune for 5 minutes, turning to brown them evenly until they're golden all the way around. Once they're cooked through, return all the tsukune to the pan with the soy sauce and mirin and let simmer for 2 minutes until hot and lightly coated in the sauce.

Serve immediately on a plate, with an egg yolk in a small bowl on the side, lightly beaten, to dip into as you eat.

Note: People with compromised immune systems are advised to avoid raw eggs.

IZAKAYA AT HOME

asari no sake mushi

sake-steamed clams

Serves 2 as a sharing plate

300g (10½oz) clams, cleaned

3 tbsp sake

2 tsp butter

½ tbsp soy sauce

handful of chives, chopped

bread, to serve (optional)

This five-minute recipe, made with just a few ingredients, pops up regularly in *izakayas*, so I felt it needed to make an appearance here. It is delicious served with bread to mop up the juices, or it can be tossed through pasta.

If the clams need to be purged (check with your fishmonger), soak them in a bowl of salted water for 30 minutes to 1 hour, then drain.

Heat the sake in a large heavy-based saucepan that has a lid over a medium-high heat. When it comes to the boil, add the clams, cover with the lid and cook for 3–4 minutes, or until all the shells have opened and the clams are cooked through. Discard any clams that remain closed.

Add the butter, soy sauce and chives and cook for a futher minute until the butter has melted.

Serve with bread for mopping up the sauce, if you like.

braised pork belly

buta no kakuni

Serves 4 as a sharing plate

500g (1lb 2oz) pork belly, rind removed

1 tbsp neutral oil, such as rapeseed (canola) or sunflower

1 leek, cut into 4 large pieces

4 eggs

1 tbsp hondashi (see page 16)

3½ tbsp soy sauce

4 tbsp sake

3 tbsp mirin

3½ tbsp sugar

3 slices fresh root ginger

steamed rice (see page 30), to serve

I was slightly intimidated the first time I thought of making slow-cooked pork belly. What if it turned gummy instead of falling apart at the touch of a chopstick? But it's actually foolproof when you use the double-boil method I use here. The first boil is just to cook the pork belly through, while the second one allows it to get properly tender and absorb all the flavours. I love to serve this with eggs that are cooked just long enough to turn the yolks jammy, then spoon lots of the delicious savoury sauce over them when serving.

Cut the pork belly into 5cm (2in) squares. Heat the oil in a pan over a medium-high heat, add the pork and sear on all sides until evenly browned. Remove with a slotted spoon and transfer to a plate.

Fill a large pan with water, add the pork and the leeks, bring to the boil, then reduce the heat and simmer uncovered for 1 hour, or until the pork is tender.

Meanwhile, bring a separate pan of water to the boil, carefully lower in the eggs and boil for 7 minutes (this will give you eggs with jammy yolks). Remove with a slotted spoon and put into a bowl filled with iced water to prevent further cooking. When cool enough to handle, peel and set aside until ready to serve.

When it is tender, drain the pork belly and leeks (discard the cooking water), then return the pork and leeks to the pan with 400ml (14fl oz/1¾ cups) water. Add the hondashi, soy sauce, sake, mirin, sugar and ginger, bring to the boil, then reduce the heat to a simmer. Scrunch up a piece of baking paper, then cut to the same size and shape as the inside of the pan (this is called a cartouche). Lay the cartouche directly onto the surface of the liquid and cook very gently for 1 hour.

You can serve immediately, or let it cool, then cover and chill in the fridge overnight. It will be even better reheated the next day, as the flavours will have had time to develop. Serve with the soft-boiled eggs, drizzling the sauce over them, and some steamed rice.

IZAKAYA AT HOME

156   IZAKAYA AT HOME

ham and cheese katsu

ham to cheese no katsu

Makes 10 (serves 4 as a sharing plate)

For the katsu

10 thick, round slices of smoked ham

60g (2¼oz) grated (shredded) mozzarella cheese

150ml (5fl oz/scant ⅔ cup) neutral oil, such as rapeseed (canola) or sunflower

For the breading

50g (1¾oz) plain (all-purpose) flour

1 egg, beaten

100g (3½oz) panko breadcrumbs

salt and freshly ground black pepper

Ham katsu is a classic old-school menu item in Japan. It's normally a thick slice of Spam that's breaded in a thick layer of panko breadcrumbs and deep-fried (yes, it's a great drinking snack). I really love making these using thinner slices of smoked ham with a surprise molten cheese element. You can use any ham you like, but I try to avoid the wafer-thin type, so it holds together better. If you stuffed this into a sandwich, it would be delicious with a slathering of mayo and some lettuce.

Wrap the ham slices around the cheese to form ten half-moon shapes. Set aside on a plate.

Get your breading station set up. Put the flour on a plate and season with salt and pepper. Put the egg in a shallow bowl and the breadcrumbs on a separate shallow plate. Dip the ham rolls first in the flour, then the egg, then finally the breadcrumbs to give them a good coating.

Heat the oil in a heavy-based frying pan (skillet). When it's good and hot, gently add the ham and cheese rolls, handling them carefully to ensure the cheese doesn't fall out. You may need to do this in batches. Fry for 2 minutes on one side, then flip using tongs and cook for a further minute on the other side.

Serve immediately, being careful of the molten cheese.

maguro no tataki

grilled tuna steak

Serves 2 as a sharing plate

150g (5½oz) sashimi-grade tuna, cut 2.5–3cm (1–1¼in) thick

1 tbsp olive oil

1 garlic clove, very finely sliced

1 tbsp sake

1 tbsp soy sauce

1 large tomato, cut into small uneven chunks

drizzle of extra-virgin olive oil

1 tsp apple cider vinegar

salt and freshly ground black pepper

There's something so impressive about a beautifully cooked tuna steak. The key is to sear it so lightly that it doesn't have a chance to cook inside and is still raw in the centre. I serve this dish as it is, but you could make it into a salad with the addition of finely sliced onions, avocado and more tomatoes.

Season the tuna with salt and pepper and set aside.

Heat the olive oil in a frying pan (skillet) over a low heat, add the garlic and fry until the slices turn a light golden colour. Remove using a slotted spoon and transfer to a plate.

Using the same pan, turn the heat up to medium-high, then add the tuna and cook for 10–15 seconds on each side until lightly browned on the outside. There's no need to rest the tuna – simply slice it on an angle and arrange it on a serving plate.

For the sauce, add the sake and soy sauce to the pan, cook over a medium heat for 1 minute, then turn the heat off. Set the sauce aside in a bowl to cool slightly.

Put the chopped tomato in a bowl, season with a bit of salt and drizzle over the extra-virgin olive oil and the vinegar.

To serve, pour the sauce over the tuna and sprinkle over the garlic and tomato chunks.

IZAKAYA AT HOME

159

butter and soy sauce scallops

hotate no butter shoyu yaki

Serves 4 as a sharing plate

1½ tbsp butter

200g (7oz) scallops (around 12 scallops), cleaned and trimmed (keep the shells if you have them)

2 tbsp soy sauce

juice of ½ lemon

20g (¾oz) chives, finely chopped

steamed rice (see page 30), to serve (optional)

If you have the chance, make this dish on a live fire, such as a barbecue or a beach fire, cooking the cleaned scallops in their shells. For an at-home dinner, buy the juiciest scallops you can and sear them ever so slightly, as I've done here.

Heat the butter in a frying pan (skillet) over a medium heat. Once the butter is foaming, add the scallops and sear for 1 minute. Turn carefully and sear for a further minute. Remove from the pan and set aside.

Add the soy sauce, lemon and chives to the pan and heat gently for 1 minute.

To serve, I often place the scallops back in their shells and then pour over the sauce, but you can also serve them with some steamed rice.

sea bream sashimi

tai no sashimi

Serves 2 as a sharing plate

100g (3½oz) sashimi-grade sea bream fillets, any pin bones removed

30g (1oz) shibazuke (pickled aubergines/eggplant), roughly chopped

1 tsp wasabi paste

1 tsp shio kombu (see page 23)

1 tbsp extra-virgin olive oil

30g (1oz) microgreens, or substitute with rocket (arugula) leaves (optional)

3 shiso leaves (optional)

½ tsp toasted sesame seeds

A light and simple sashimi dish. I love using shio kombu (dried salted kelp flakes seasoned with soy sauce and sugar) to flavour things, as it gives a savoury umami-ness to a dish. Shibazuke is a type of pickled aubergine (eggplant) that is pickled with shiso (a Japanese herb similar to basil or fresh coriander/cilantro), so it has a very savoury and light basil taste. It can be bought at any Japanese supermarket and provides an element of crunch as well as saltiness. You could easily make this without the greens, and it would be great served with steamed rice.

Slice the fish on an angle into 2–3mm ($1/16$–$1/8$in) slices. Transfer to a bowl.

Add the shibazuke to the bowl along with the wasabi, shio kombu, olive oil, micro greens and shiso leaves, if using. Mix gently, then arrange on a plate and sprinkle over the sesame seeds.

IZAKAYA AT HOME 163

164　　　　　　　　　　　　　　　　　　　　　　　　　　　　IZAKAYA AT HOME

octopus sashimi

taco to ponzu no sashimi

Serves 2 as a sharing plate

For the octopus

120g (4¼oz) cooked octopus

3 shiso leaves (a Japanese herb reminiscent of basil), finely sliced, or substitute with fresh coriander (cilantro)

20g (¾oz) full-fat cream cheese, cut into cubes

For the dressing

1 tbsp extra-virgin olive oil

1 tsp lemon juice

1 small garlic clove, finely grated

1 tsp ponzu (see page 22)

flaky salt and freshly ground black pepper

This is a very simple small plate to serve alongside drinks. It's got elements of Japanese flavours from the citrussy ponzu and shiso leaves, but has an unexpected touch from the extra-virgin olive oil and cream cheese. It's super addictive. I love using cream cheese here, but you could use mozzarella or any mild, milky cheese.

I'd recommend getting a pack of ready-cooked and prepared octopus with no extra seasoning from Greek and Spanish delis, so that you don't have to go to the effort of cooking octopus at home.

Slice the octopus into bite-sized chunks and put in a bowl.

Combine the dressing ingredients in a separate bowl, then add the dressing to the octopus along with the shiso leaves or fresh coriander. Mix thoroughly, then add the cream cheese and give it a light toss.

Serve immediately.

sweet-and-salty chicken wings

amakara tebasaki

Serves 2 as a sharing plate

For the wings

500g (1lb 2oz) chicken wings

salt and freshly ground black pepper

For the sauce

3 tbsp soy sauce

2 tbsp mirin

2 tbsp sugar

1 garlic clove, finely grated

2cm (¾in) piece of fresh root ginger, finely grated

1 tsp sesame seeds

pinch of chilli flakes

To serve

finely chopped chives (optional)

What's better than lip-smackingly delicious chicken wings? They are the ultimate drinking snack. This version has two benefits: first of all, they're grilled (broiled), not fried, which means less cleaning up; and second of all, you can quite easily make the wings in advance, then reheat and glaze before serving. The sauce is sweet and salty with a little spicy kick, so they are quite perfectly balanced in every way.

Pat the chicken wings dry using paper towels, then season with salt and pepper and put on a flat baking sheet.

Preheat the grill (broiler) to 220°C (425°F). When ready, put the chicken wings under the grill and cook for 5 minutes on one side, then carefully flip and cook for a further 7 minutes. Flip them again and grill for a final 3 minutes. You want to cook them for 15 minutes in total, or until the wings are completely cooked through.

While the wings are cooking, put all the sauce ingredients in a frying pan (skillet) set over a medium heat. Simmer until it's reduced to a thick and sticky sauce (this should take 4–5 minutes), then turn the heat off.

Add the wings to the pan of sauce and coat them evenly for a minute or so – you want the wings to be covered in the sauce, but retain their crisp skin.

Serve immediately on a warmed platter and top with chopped chives, if you like.

cucumber umeboshi salad

kyuri to ume no salada

Serves 4 as a sharing plate

V + VG

1 large cucumber (150g/5½oz), unpeeled

1 umeboshi (see page 24)

1 tsp toasted sesame oil

1 tsp soy sauce

1 tsp apple cider vinegar

½ tsp sugar

2 shiso leaves (a Japanese herb reminiscent of basil), finely sliced, or use a small bunch of fresh coriander (cilantro) leaves (optional)

salt

The star of the show in this refreshing, crunchy salad is the sweet-and-sour umeboshi (pickled salted plum), which provides flavour and tang. Think of this as smacked cucumber salad's cool cousin. If you can get your hands on shiso leaves, they add a lovely fragrant flavour, but fresh coriander (cilantro) is also fine. This is delicious as is, or serve it on top of tofu.

Put the cucumber on a solid, secured chopping board. Using a rolling pin, whack the cucumber a few times until it's crushed and slightly flattened. Pull the flesh apart and cut it into uneven bite-sized pieces. Sprinkle with salt and put in a colander set over a bowl for about 10–15 minutes to drain off the excess liquid.

Meanwhile, crush the umeboshi in a bowl with the back of a spoon to form a paste, then mix in the sesame oil, soy sauce, apple cider vinegar and sugar.

Rinse the drained cucumber to remove the salt, then pat dry with paper towels. Put in a serving bowl and mix in the dressing, along with the shiso or fresh coriander. Leave to sit for 15 minutes before serving.

kimchi and tuna otsumami

kimchi to maguro no otsumami

Serves 4 as a snack

150g (5½oz) sashimi-grade tuna steaks, or 2 cans of tuna, drained

70g (2½oz) kimchi, chopped

1 tsp toasted sesame seeds

1 tsp ponzu (see page 22)

1 tsp toasted sesame oil

To serve

8 shiso leaves (a Japanese herb reminiscent of basil), or top with fresh coriander (cilantro)

1 sheet of nori, cut into 8 rectangles

steamed rice (see page 30; optional)

In Japan, the selection of small dishes you're served with evening drinks is called *otsumami*. This dish is punchy and loaded with texture and is great on its own or served with steamed rice for a more complete meal. If it's handier, you could use canned tuna rather than raw for a different flavour.

Slice the tuna into 2cm (¾in) cubes and put in a bowl. Add the kimchi, sesame seeds, ponzu and sesame oil and mix gently.

Serve immediately on a plate or in a shallow bowl with shiso leaves or fresh coriander scattered on top. Use the nori rectangles to wrap the tuna/kimchi mixture and eat it in single mouthfuls. Serve with steamed rice, if you like.

IZAKAYA AT HOME

chicken thighs with ponzu sauce

tori momo no ponzu sauce

Serves 4 as a sharing plate

For the chicken

¼ red onion

2 boneless chicken thighs (skin on)

1 tbsp neutral oil, such as rapeseed (canola) or sunflower

1 tbsp sake

salt and freshly ground black pepper

For the sauce

1 tbsp mayonnaise

1 tbsp yuzu ponzu (see page 22)

1 small garlic clove, finely grated

freshly ground black pepper, to taste

To serve

finely chopped chives (optional)

steamed rice (see page 30; optional)

This simple chicken dish is all about the sauce: creamy, well rounded and with a bit of zing from the citrussy-sharp yuzu ponzu. Be generous with the black pepper to add a bit of heat.

Slice the onion very finely, then put in a small bowl of iced water for the duration of the cooking process.

Season the chicken thighs with salt and pepper.

Heat the oil in a lidded frying pan (skillet) over a medium heat. When hot, add the thighs, skin-side down. Cook, without disturbing, for 5 minutes until the skin is browned and crispy, then flip the chicken over using tongs. Cook for a further 3–4 minutes until the undersides are browned, then add the sake to the pan and cover with the lid. Cook the chicken over a medium-low heat for 2–3 minutes until the sake has evaporated and the chicken is completely cooked through.

Transfer the chicken to a chopping board and keep warm while you make the sauce. Combine the mayonnaise, yuzu ponzu, garlic and pepper in a bowl.

Slice the chicken into bite-sized chunks and arrange on a serving plate. Drain the onions and pat dry, then scatter them over the chicken. Serve with the sauce on the side, top with the chopped chives, if using, and enjoy with steamed rice, if you like.

scallop carpaccio with strawberries

hotate to ichigo no carpaccio

Serves 2 as a sharing plate

150g (5½oz) sashimi-grade scallops, cleaned and trimmed (roes removed)

½ tsp salt

50g (1¾oz) strawberries

4 radishes

small handful of torn parsley leaves (optional)

For the dressing

1 tbsp extra-virgin olive oil

1 tsp white wine vinegar

pinch each sugar and salt

freshly ground black pepper

This is a quintessential summer dish that I put together because it makes the most of the season's beautiful ingredients. The sweet, tender scallops work magic with ripe strawberries and peppery radishes. The dressing is so simple and the dish requires just a few ingredients, so I recommend getting the very best you can find.

Put the scallops in a shallow bowl, scatter over the salt and let them sit for 10 minutes.

Rinse away the salt and pat the scallops dry with paper towels. Slice them into thin rounds and lay on a serving platter. Finely slice the strawberries and radishes and arrange them on the platter with the scallops.

Combine the dressing ingredients in a small bowl and drizzle over. Scatter with the parsley, if using, and serve.

IZAKAYA AT HOME

stir-fried chicken with radishes

tori to kabu no itame

Serves 4 as a sharing plate

1 tbsp olive oil

150g (5½oz) boneless chicken thighs, cut into bite-sized chunks

300g (10½oz) radishes, cut in half, or turnips, cut into quarters

2 tbsp mentsuyu (see page 18)

1 tbsp shio kombu (see page 23)

2 tsp butter

steamed rice (see page 30), to serve (optional)

Wherever I travel, radishes and turnips seem to be underrated. They're actually fantastic for taking on the flavours of any dish – in this case, chicken and the savoury tastes of shio kombu (dried salted kelp flakes) and mentsuyu (a soy and dashi sauce). Butter's not really optional in this dish, as it really rounds out the flavours, making it incredibly moreish. This would also be great served with rice, if you were looking for a more substantial dish.

Heat 2 teaspoons of the olive oil in a frying pan (skillet) over a medium heat. When hot, place the chicken pieces in the pan, skin-side down, and cook for 3 minutes on each side, or until they are completely cooked through (the flesh will be opaque, the juices will run clear and no pink meat will remain). Remove with a slotted spoon and set aside.

Wipe the pan clean with a paper towel and heat the remaining teaspoon of oil over a medium-high heat. Add the radishes or turnips and let them brown on each side, turning to cook them evenly. This should take 2–3 minutes.

Return the chicken pieces to the pan, adding the mentsuyu, shio kombu and butter, and cook for a further minute over a medium heat until everything is well incorporated.

Serve straight away, with steamed rice, if you like.

pork belly with thick fried tofu

butabara and atsuage

Serves 2 as a sharing plate

1 tbsp neutral oil, such as rapeseed (canola) or sunflower

200g (7oz) thinly sliced pork belly, cut into 6–7cm (2½–2¾in) pieces

200g (7oz) atsuage tofu (thick fried tofu), cut into 5cm (2in) cubes

1 tsp hondashi (see page 16)

1½ tbsp soy sauce

1½ tbsp mirin

1½ tsp sugar

To serve

2 spring onions (scallions), finely sliced

shichimi togarashi (see page 23)

A simple *izakaya* dish that is comforting and perfectly balanced. Although it's just tofu and pork, it has a rich flavour that cries out for an ice-cold beer. Don't skimp on the shichimi togarashi when it comes to serving. This spice blend is made up of seven (*shichi*) spices: usually ground red chilli peppers, yuzu peel or orange peel, ginger, red chilli, black and white sesame, sansho (Japanese peppercorns) – and it adds the citrussy flavour and chilli hit you'll want.

Atsuage is thick fried tofu, the sister of aburaage, thin fried tofu pockets. Atsuage soaks up flavours well while holding its shape when cooked. You can find it in the fridge section of Asian supermarkets, or you can make it yourself: cover a block of firm tofu with paper towels, put a weight (such as a can of beans) on top and leave for 15 minutes to press out excess moisture. Fry it in neutral oil (use enough so that the oil goes up at least halfway up the tofu) for 5–6 minutes until it's browned on all sides. Drain on a wire rack and it's ready to use.

Heat the oil in a frying pan (skillet) over a medium-high heat, add the pork and cook, stirring, for 2–3 minutes until lightly browned. Set aside in a bowl.

Fry the tofu cubes in the same pan until warmed through and browned all over, around 3–4 minutes, then set aside in the same bowl as the pork.

Using paper towels, wipe the pan clean, then add 150ml (5fl oz/ scant ⅔ cup) water along with the hondashi, soy sauce, mirin and sugar. Let it simmer over a low-medium heat until small bubbles rise to the surface, about 2 minutes, then add the pork and tofu and give it a stir. Simmer until the sauce has reduced by a quarter (you don't want it to be too thick).

Serve in a shallow bowl topped with spring onions and a sprinkle of shichimi togarashi.

the ultimate potato salad

potato salada

Serves 4 as a sharing plate

½ white onion

1 cucumber

300g (10½oz) potatoes, cut into quarters

½ carrot (80g/2¾oz), quartered lengthways and cut into 3mm (⅛in) slices

1 tsp sugar

1 tbsp apple cider vinegar

½ x 400g (14oz) can of sweetcorn (corn)

40g (1½oz) smoked ham

5 tbsp mayonnaise, or more as needed

salt and freshly ground black pepper

1 soft-boiled egg, halved, to serve

There's nothing better than a chunky potato salad filled with a treasure-trove of ingredients. Japanese potato salad has an array of crunchy vegetables and smoky ham, and is gently mashed, so it's smoother than its Western counterparts. It is delicious. Use any leftovers for a potato salad sandwich the next day: just use white bread, generously buttered, and fill it.

Finely slice the onion using a knife or mandoline and put in a bowl of iced water. Let it sit while you prepare the rest of the recipe.

Finely slice the cucumber and put it in a separate bowl with two good pinches of salt. Set aside while you cook the potatoes. The salt will draw out the excess water.

Put the potatoes in a large pan of cold salted water over a high heat. Bring to the boil, then reduce the heat to medium. Cook the potatoes for 10 minutes, then add the sliced carrot. Cook for a further 5 minutes, or until the potatoes are tender when tested with a fork.

Drain the potatoes and carrots and transfer to a bowl, adding the sugar and vinegar. Season with salt, then crush the potatoes with the back of a fork until crumbly. Leave to cool.

Meanwhile, drain the corn and cut the ham into bite-sized chunks. Drain the onion, then rinse the cucumbers and squeeze as much liquid from them as you can. Set aside with the corn and ham.

Once the potatoes are cool, gently mix in the mayonnaise, then all the add-ins. Taste and season with black pepper and more mayonnaise if needed. Serve in a bowl, topped with a soft-boiled egg.

IZAKAYA AT HOME 179

IZAKAYA AT HOME

fried fishcakes

isobeage

Serves 4 as a sharing plate

5 chikuwa, defrosted if frozen, at room temperature

5 okra, tops trimmed, or use asparagus spears in season

150ml (5fl oz/scant 2/3 cup) neutral oil, such as rapeseed (canola) or sunflower, for frying

For the batter

3 tbsp plain (all-purpose) flour

1 tsp aonori (see page 23; optional)

3 tbsp cold sparkling water

pinch of salt

To serve

lemon wedges

mayonnaise

chilli oil

Isobeage is one of the more common *izakaya* snacks in which chikuwa, a type of Japanese fishcake, are fried in batter and served with mayo. These bouncy, light fishcakes are different from the breaded and deep-fried ones you'd find in the supermarket. The fish is minced (ground) and wrapped around bamboo skewers, then steamed, which creates a hole in the centre. They're often eaten as fried snacks, holes stuffed with cucumber, and served with mayo.

You can find chikuwa in the fridge or frozen section of Japanese supermarkets or buy them online. They've got a very light texture and a taste that's not too oily or overpowering. I've stuffed them with okra, but you could also use asparagus for a nice twist. The batter is usually made with aonori (finely milled seaweed), but you could leave it out if you don't have it.

Fill the hole of each chikuwa piece with the okra. Slice each filled piece on an angle into 3 even pieces (you will have 15 pieces in total).

For the batter, mix the flour, aonori (if using) and salt in a large bowl, then gently stir in the water. Don't overmix or it will become claggy and heavy when shallow-fried.

Heat the oil in a frying pan (skillet) over a medium heat. When the oil is hot, briefly dip the chikuwa pieces in the batter to lightly coat. Working in batches, carefully add the battered chikuwa to the hot oil and fry for 3 minutes, turning so all sides get browned. Drain on a wire rack set over a plate and keep warm while you cook the rest.

Serve straight away, with lemon wedges and mayonnaise with a dollop of chilli oil on top.

agedashi nasu

dashi-marinated aubergines

Serves 2 as a sharing plate

VO + VGO

1 tbsp hondashi or vegan alternative (see page 16)

1 tbsp soy sauce

1 tbsp mirin

5 small aubergines (eggplants) (100g/3½oz each), tops trimmed

150ml (5fl oz/scant ⅔ cup) neutral oil, such as rapeseed (canola) or sunflower

To serve

finely grated fresh root ginger

daikon orishi (finely grated daikon radish)

steamed rice (see page 30)

This is a great recipe to enjoy alongside fried dishes such as Karaage (fried chicken; see page 149) or katsu (fried pork fillet; see page 84). Although the aubergine (eggplant) is initially fried, most of the oil is later removed and the aubergine is then marinated in a light dashi-based broth that does away with any trace of oiliness. It is topped with grated ginger and daikon, which brighten the finished dish.

Heat 100ml (3½fl oz/scant ½ cup) of water with the hondashi, soy sauce and mirin in a pan until almost boiling. Reduce the heat and let it simmer for 2–3 minutes, then take off the heat and set aside to cool.

Meanwhile, slice the aubergines in half lengthways (the pieces should be small enough that each can be eaten in a couple of bites). Using a sharp knife, cut small, closely spaced incisions in the skin, so the dashi can soak into them, being careful not to cut all the way through – see the photograph.

Heat the oil in a heavy-based pan. When hot, working in batches, add the aubergine pieces and shallow-fry, stirring gently, until lightly browned all over and softened, around 5 minutes. Remove with a slotted spoon and transfer to a plate.

Heat 500ml (17fl oz/2 cups plus 2 tablespoons) water in a pan until boiling and set aside. Once all the aubergine pieces are cooked, put them in a colander in the sink and pour the hot water over them to remove most of the oil. Transfer the drained aubergines to the pan with the dashi mixture and set aside for at least 1 hour.

Serve at room temperature, topped with small mounds of grated ginger and daikon oroshi, with steamed rice.

IZAKAYA AT HOME

cucumber and shio kombu salad

kyuri to shio kombu salada

Serves 2 as a sharing plate

V + VG

2 Japanese or Turkish cucumbers, or 4 baby cucumbers, unpeeled

2 tbsp shio kombu (see page 23)

1 tbsp toasted sesame oil

1 tsp toasted sesame seeds

½ tsp chilli flakes

A good cucumber salad is the best accompaniment to a drink. This crunchy version is incredibly savoury from the shio kombu (dried salted kelp seasoned with soy sauce and sugar) and has a bit of a chilli kick. Try to get your hands on Japanese or Turkish cucumbers if you can – both have a thin skin, fewer seeds and are crunchier than standard English cucumbers. Otherwise, baby cucumbers work better than the large ones, which tend to be quite watery. Make this thirty minutes before serving, so you can chill it in the fridge and the shio kombu can soften as it sits.

Put the cucumbers on a solid, secured chopping board. Using a rolling pin, whack them a few times until slightly flattened. Pull the flesh apart and cut into uneven bite-sized pieces.

In a bowl, mix the cucumbers, shio kombu, toasted sesame oil, toasted sesame seeds and chilli flakes. Massage it all together with your hands – you want to soften the shio kombu as you mix it. Cover and chill in the fridge for 30 minutes, then serve.

marinated eggs

ajitsuke tamago

Makes 4

V

4 medium eggs, at room temperature

3 tbsp sake

3 tbsp mirin

3 tbsp soy sauce

1 tbsp sugar

½ tbsp toasted sesame oil

1 garlic clove, finely grated

½ tsp vegetable stock powder

These savoury and sweet eggs make a brilliant snack, and they're great to have in your fridge to make a meal – serve them on top of rice, with noodles or to top a potato salad. They take less than ten minutes to prepare plus an hour chilling in the fridge and they're ready. They'll last a couple of days, but I recommend eating them within the first 24 hours or the flavour can get too salty. These would make great devilled eggs – just marinate them for a few hours, then cut them in half, scoop out the yolk, mix it with mayonnaise, stuff back into the whites and top with a sprinkle of shichimi togarashi for a savoury and spicy kick.

Bring a pan of water to the boil. Carefully lower in the eggs, reduce the heat to medium-low and cook for 7 minutes.

While the eggs are boiling, make the marinade. Put the remaining ingredients in a small pan, bring to the boil, then reduce the heat and let it simmer for 1 minute, making sure the sugar has dissolved. Transfer the marinade to a bowl or sealable plastic container.

At the end of their cooking time, drain the eggs and transfer to a bowl of iced water to stop them cooking further. When cool enough to handle, peel them, then put them in the marinade. Leave them to marinate for at least 1 hour, turning halfway through.

Store, covered, in the fridge for up to 2 days if you're not eating them straight away.

IZAKAYA AT HOME

corn tempura

toumorokoshi tempura

Makes 10 (serves 2 as a snack)

V + VG

150g (5½oz) sweetcorn (corn), from 2 cobs/ears of corn; or use canned corn, drained

handful of parsley leaves (optional)

4 tbsp plain (all-purpose) flour

pinch of salt

400ml (14fl oz/1¾ cups) neutral oil, such as rapeseed (canola) or sunflower

flaky salt, to serve

The sweet joys of summer in a bite. These crunchy morsels are truly my favourite tempura – and they're as simple as just sweetcorn, deep-fried in a light batter and sprinkled with salt. If you fancied it, you could add a handful of parsley leaves to the batter with the corn before frying.

A cooking thermometer would be useful for this recipe.

Using a sharp knife, cutting away from you on a secure work surface, slice the corn kernels from the cobs. (If using canned corn, just skip this step.)

Put the corn kernels (and the parsley leaves, if using) in a bowl and add the flour and salt. Mix well so all the kernels are covered in flour, then add 2 tablespoons of water and mix gently. Don't overmix or it will become heavy and claggy when fried.

To fry, heat the oil in a large, heavy-based pan filled no more than halfway and let it come to 170°C (340°F). If you don't have a thermometer, dip the tip of a wooden or bamboo chopstick into the oil. When it's hot enough, a steady stream of small air bubbles will rise to the surface. Working in batches, carefully drop in heaped tablespoonfuls of the batter. You will have enough for 10 balls.

Cook, turning, until golden brown all over, 3–4 minutes. Remove with a slotted spoon and drain on a rack set over a plate to get rid of any excess oil. Keep them warm while you cook the rest.

Sprinkle with flaky salt and serve straight away.

tori to cheese no gyoza

flat gyoza with chicken and cheese

Serves 2 as a snack

1 tsp neutral oil, such as rapeseed (canola) or sunflower

12 gyoza wrappers

150g (5½ oz) minced (ground) chicken

4 shiso leaves (a Japanese herb reminiscent of basil), finely sliced (optional)

50g (1¾oz) grated (shredded) mozzarella

salt and freshly ground black pepper

This is a snack I made for myself one night when I was cleaning out bits in the fridge, and was craving something hot and cheesy that would be great with a beer. It's made with ready-made gyoza wrappers, so it's much easier than making gyoza from scratch – and because it's flat (a bit like a quesadilla), there's no need for folding and pleating. I've used chicken mince (ground chicken) here, but you could use up any leftover meat in your fridge and add any cheese you have to hand. Savoury, crunchy and delicious.

You will find gyoza wrappers (also sold as gyoza dumpling wrappers or gyoza skins) in the freezer section of Asian supermarkets. They are circular, made from wheat flour and sold in packs of twenty-five or fifty. Be careful not to mistake them for wonton wrappers, which are square and made with egg, giving them a yellow hue.

Cook these cheesy gyozas in two batches.

Heat the oil in a lidded frying pan (skillet) over a medium heat. Place three gyoza wrappers in the base of the pan and top each with a sixth of the chicken mince, flattening it down with your fingers and seasoning with a pinch of salt and pepper. Top each with a sixth of the shiso leaves, if using, and a sixth of the cheese, then top each with a gyoza wrapper to cover the filling completely.

Put the lid on the pan and cook for 3 minutes until the undersides are golden brown, then carefully flip over and cook for a further 2–3 minutes until nicely browned on the other side.

Repeat with the remaining gyoza wrappers and fillings and serve straight away.

IZAKAYA AT HOME

cod's roe and potato harumaki

mentaiko to potato no harumaki

Makes 20 (serves 6 as
a sharing plate)

VO

250g (9oz) potatoes, peeled
and quartered

1 tbsp mayonnaise

45g (1^2/$_3$oz) mentaiko (see page 18)

65g (2¼oz) grated (shredded)
mozzarella (vegetarian, if necessary)

3 shiso leaves (a Japanese herb
reminiscent of basil), roughly torn
(optional)

a few twists of black pepper

1 tbsp plain (all-purpose) flour

5 spring roll wrappers
(each 22 x 22cm/8½ x 8½in)

5 tbsp neutral oil, such as rapeseed
(canola) or sunflower

sweet chilli sauce or chilli oil,
to serve (optional)

These crunchy snacks are incredibly crispy and light on the outside and filled with a potato filling that's deliciously savoury and moreish. I've used mentaiko (smoked cod's roe) but you could, of course, leave this out if you're vegetarian and just amp up the shiso (and use vegetarian mozzarella).

Put the potatoes in a pan of boiling water. Cook for 15 minutes, or until tender in the middle when tested with the tip of a sharp knife. Drain and crush with a fork – you want to retain some texture, not make a smooth mash. Set aside to cool, then gently mix in the mayonnaise, mentaiko, mozzarella, shiso and pepper.

Make a 'glue' to seal the wrappers by combining the flour with 2 tablespoons of water in a bowl until the mixture has a sticky consistency. Put the spring roll wrappers in a single stack and cut into 20 long rectangles.

Starting with a single rectangle, with the shorter side facing you, put 1½ tablespoons of the filling onto the bottom left corner, then fold it up to the facing corner. Fold again to enclose the filling, then continue folding and wrapping, forming a neat triangular parcel. Brush the edges with the flour and water mixture to form a seal. Set aside and continue with the remaining filling and wrappers.

To shallow-fry, heat 3 tablespoons of the oil in a frying pan (skillet) over a medium-high heat. When hot, add four of the triangles and cook for 2 minutes. Carefully turn using tongs, and cook for a further 2 minutes on the other side until golden all over. Transfer the cooked parcels to a wire rack set over a plate to allow the excess oil to drip off. Keep warm while you cook the remaining parcels, adding more oil as needed.

Serve straight away, with sweet chilli sauce or chilli oil, if you like.

dashimaki tamago

rolled egg omelette

Serves 2 as a sharing plate

V

3 eggs, beaten

1 tbsp soy sauce

1 tbsp sugar

½ tsp hondashi or vegetarian alternative (see page 16)

1 tsp neutral oil, such as rapeseed (canola) or sunflower

To serve

5cm (2in) piece of daikon, finely grated

a drizzle of soy sauce

This is one egg dish that I needed to include in this book – eggs are whisked with dashi and a bit of soy sauce and sugar to make a really fluffy rolled omelette. This is one of those practical dishes than can be made in advance and just served at room temperature. The most authentic way to serve this is with a little mound of grated daikon oroshi and a drizzle of soy sauce on the side.

In Japan, this omelette is cooked in a purpose-made square or rectangular omelette pan called a *tamagoyaki*. If you have one, great, but you can use a regular non-stick frying pan (skillet), if not.

Whisk the eggs, soy sauce, sugar, hondashi and 3½ tablespoons of water in a bowl until very well incorporated.

Heat the oil in a *tamagoyaki* pan or frying pan (skillet) over a medium-low heat and use a paper towel to spread it evenly over the base of the pan, wiping off the excess. Keep the oiled paper towel to hand, as you will need to lightly brush the pan with oil between cooking each layer.

Add a quarter of the egg mixture to the pan, rotating it to fully cover the base in a thin layer. When the egg is mostly set and the edges starting to come away from the pan (about 2 minutes), it's time to fold. Using a spatula, fold the omelette over itself, folding it towards you two or three times so it has several layers. It will have a rectangular shape if you're using a *tamagoyaki* pan, but if you're using a regular frying pan, you will have a round-shaped omelette.

Pushing the egg roll to the back of the pan, wipe the base of the pan with the oil-soaked paper towel and add another quarter of the egg mixture, making sure to slightly lift the egg roll you just made so that the mixture can slip underneath. Once this layer is mostly cooked, roll it up again so that the new egg layer is added to the first roll.

Repeat twice more with the remaining egg mixture.

Once all the egg mixture is cooked, if you want to neaten the shape, you can wrap the roll in cling film (plastic wrap) and use a sushi mat to roll it.

Mix the grated daikon and soy sauce in a small bowl. Serve the omelette at room temperature with the daikon oroshi on the side.

IZAKAYA AT HOME

the izakaya 居酒屋

'*Irasshaimase!*' ('Welcome!') is the greeting you'll hear as you enter a smoke-filled and bustling *izakaya* in town: no matter whether you're in the heart of Shibuya or in an alleyway in Kobe, you'll be able to find a spot in which to drink and eat to your heart's content while surrounded by locals and in the midst of the flurry of service. This may feel like an episode of *The Bear* – waiters running around and dropping off plates to tables, pouring yet another lemon sour and loud voices saying '*Suimasen*' ('Excuse me') – but you've got to get in there and be ready.

Izakaya culture is well known around the world. The idea of a pub, bar or tavern that serves drinks but no food seems funny to people living in Japan: a place to drink, yet no simmered fish or cucumbers with miso? It's the complete opposite of what you'll get at an *izakaya*.

Of course, you've got to get your drinks in first. Shout '*Nama kudasai*' for an ice-cold draught beer. Two minutes into sitting down, you'll be presented with *otoshi* – a small bite to whet your appetite with your drink. As you look around the room, you'll see plenty of menu items, more likely than not scribbled in Japanese. So, if you can't read Japanese, here is your guide to the *izakaya* menu.

Gyoza (and sometimes sui gyoza) 餃子
Beer and gyoza (pan-fried dumplings) go hand in hand. I mean, the combination of ice-cold effervescent beer paired with juicy, meaty, crispy dumplings: perfection. Sui gyoza (boiled dumplings) will be on the menu every now and again. They will be served hot and steaming. Douse them in chilli oil, soy sauce and vinegar and slurp up.

Gyusuji nikomi 牛すじ煮込み
I was wrong about this slow-simmered beef dish for so long, thinking that it would be boring and maybe filled with stringy bits of meat. I was missing out on a dish made with such time, care and craftsmanship. It's cooked for hours over a low flame. In it, you'll find chunks of beef, gobo (burdock root) and carrots, and sometimes the odd piece of aburaage (fried tofu). One thing's for certain, though – the meat produces the most beautiful and gentle stock. A must-order dish, winter or summer!

Karaage 唐揚げ
It goes without saying, but fried chicken is the one thing not to miss in Japan. Whether it's Famichiki, Family Mart's own little hand-held fried chicken, or a local butcher's take on karaage, the one place you can always order it fresh and cooked to order is at a busy *izakaya*. You'll be presented with a mountain of chicken thighs that have been marinated to the heavens, served with a big wedge of lemon to squeeze over, mayo and – if you're lucky – some grated daikon oroshi, too.

Negitoro ネギトロ
This is tuna cut into chunks or finely minced into a paste, mixed with finely chopped spring onions. Grab a piece of crunchy nori (crisp dried seaweed) and spread over a bit of wasabi and a dollop of negitoro. Dip into soy sauce and you have the perfect bite.

Potato salad ポテサラ
Japanese potato salad is a must every time you go out. It's normally combined with ham, corn and cucumbers and is sometimes topped with a marinated soft-boiled egg, fried wonton skins or a drizzle of crispy chilli oil. The world's your oyster with this one, and every place will have their own take on it, so it's worth exploring every single one.

Otsukemono お漬物
You'll probably want something fresh or pickly to cut through the drinks and all the food. Otsukemono (pickled or preserved vegetables) are it. The selection will be different at every *izakaya*. Maybe you'll have takuan (daikon radish), yamaimo (mountain yam) or nasu (aubergine/eggplant). They'll be salty, maybe a bit spicy and very cold and crunchy. Look out for tataki kyuri: smacked cucumbers massaged with shio kombu (dried, salted, seasoned kelp) or crunchy chilli oil.

Yakitori 焼き鳥
You'll spot the scented smoke coming off the *hibachi* grill from a mile away as these skewers of chicken are grilled. A few must-tries for people new to the world of yakitori are:

Kawa かわ
The skewered chicken skin is salted to perfection and it has a bit of smokiness from the grill, with a variety of textures. If there was an ultimate pairing for beer, this would be it.

Nankotsu 軟骨
For the adventurous eaters out there, skewered, grilled chicken cartilage is eaten more for its texture than its flavour. You'll also often find the cartilage fried in batter, but served this way you get more texture and crunch as you bite through.

Negima ねぎま
One of the most popular items at any yakitori spot, this is chicken thigh with leeks, skewered and grilled. The sweetness of the leeks comes out when charred on the grill and the chicken thigh is cooked until bouncy and juicy.

Tebasaki 手羽先
A chicken wing that's been butterflied so it lays flat on the stick. The skin crisps up and slightly chars and the meat is tender and juicy. A simple sprinkle of salt, shichimi togarashi (a dried spice blend spiked with chilli) and a good squeeze of lemon is all you need.

Tsukune つくね
A meatball made with minced chicken meat and often cartilage for a bit of texture. Soft and bouncy, this one should be eaten with tare – a sweet and slightly savoury sauce that the yakitori has been dipped into while grilling. Sometimes served with an egg yolk; if so, dip right in!

desserts

デザート

Japan does have a sweet culture, although traditionally it's centred around the likes of sweet red-bean soups and manju (steamed buns filled with sweetened red bean paste), rather than super-sugary offerings. In recent years, however, so many desserts have been inspired by the Western world, with more cakes and custard- or cream-forward desserts turning up on shop shelves and in home kitchens. It wasn't easy to narrow down which desserts to include here, but I've opted for practicality.

I've gone for uncomplicated recipes with accessible ingredients, and they're all certified crowd-pleasers, from the nostalgic Purin (Japanese flan; see page 207) to the Mille Crêpe Cake (layered crêpe cake; see page 200), which go down a treat every single time and take very little effort. There are a few desserts that have been inspired by Japanese ingredients and given a Western twist, too – Banana Tempura to Miso Caramel (fried bananas with miso caramel; see page 203) and Matcha to Choco no Cookies (matcha and white chocolate biscuits; see page 208). As mentioned before, Japanese kitchens don't tend to have ovens, so there are plenty of no-bake desserts, too, in hopes that anyone, anywhere can make a few of these.

Get a pot of sencha tea brewing and the desserts on the table, because no meal is complete without something a little sweet.

layered crêpe cake

mille crêpe cake

Serves 6

V

For the crêpes

450ml (16fl oz/2 cups) whole milk

4 eggs, lightly beaten

2 tbsp neutral oil, such as rapeseed (canola) or sunflower, plus 1 tsp to cook the crêpes

200g (7oz/1½ cups) plain (all-purpose) flour

For the strawberry filling

500g (1lb 2oz) strawberries, sliced into quarters

2 tbsp white caster (superfine) sugar

1 tsp lemon juice

pinch of salt

For the whipped cream and topping

250ml (9fl oz/1 cup) double (heavy) cream

½ tsp vanilla extract

icing (confectioners') sugar, to dust

This is a no-bake cake that's ready in under an hour, which can be made ahead and chilled in the fridge until ready to serve. Mille crêpe cakes are an incredibly popular dessert option in Japan, as most homes don't have an oven. This cake looks impressive, and the compôte is great if your strawberries are past their peak. You could also make this using matcha (green tea powder): simply add a teaspoon of matcha to the crêpe batter to create a rich green colour that looks beautiful against the deep-red compôte and white cream.

For the crêpes, combine the milk, eggs, 2 tablespoons of oil and 100ml (3½fl oz/scant ½ cup) water in a bowl. Slowly add the flour, tablespoon by tablespoon, whisking between additions until you have a smooth batter. Set aside to rest for 30 minutes.

Meanwhile, make the filling. Put the strawberries, sugar, lemon juice and salt in a pan set over a medium heat. Cook, stirring, until the mixture is just bubbling, then reduce the heat to medium-low and cook for 10 minutes until it's a vibrant red and has a jammy appearance. Set aside to cool to room temperature.

Whisk the cream and vanilla in a large bowl until medium-firm peaks form when the whisk is removed. Cover and leave in the fridge until you're ready to assemble the cake.

To make the crêpes, heat the teaspoon of oil in a non-stick pan over a medium heat. When hot, add a ladleful of batter, swirling it around to cover the base and just up past the bottom edge of the pan. Immediately reduce the heat to medium-low. This first crêpe will be the base of the cake on which you'll build up the layers and forms the top of the cake when serving, so it needs to have a slightly larger circumference than the rest of the crêpes. Cook for 2 minutes on one side, then carefully flip with a spatula and cook for 1 minute on the other. You want the crêpes to be pale and malleable, so don't fry them for too long. Transfer to a plate and cover with a clean dish towel.

Add another ladleful of batter to the pan, but swirl it just around the base, not up the sides, and cook as above. Continue this way until all the batter is used up. You will have enough batter for around 15 crêpes.

When you're ready to assemble the cake, put a large piece of cling film (plastic wrap) on a plate (use one that's a few inches larger that the crêpes). The cling film should have plenty of overhang. Put the largest crêpe on first and spread a thin layer of whipped cream over it, followed by thin a layer of jam (a flexible spatula is useful here). Add another crêpe and start to build up the layers, alternating the crêpe, cream and jam layers, finishing with a crêpe on top. Once the layers are complete, securely wrap the cake in cling film.

Leave the cake in the fridge to set for 3 hours. When you're ready to serve, carefully upturn the cake onto a large serving plate. Dust with icing sugar to finish and slice.

DESSERTS

DESSERTS

fried bananas with miso caramel

banana tempura to miso caramel

Serves 4

V

For the caramel

150g (5½oz/¾ cup) white caster (superfine) sugar

100ml (3½fl oz/scant ½ cup) single (light) cream

1 tbsp brown miso

2 tsp salted butter

For the bananas

2 bananas

150ml (5fl oz/scant ⅔ cup) neutral oil, such as rapeseed (canola) or sunflower

2½ tbsp rice flour

For the cinnamon sprinkle

1 tsp ground cinnamon

1 tbsp white caster (superfine) sugar

pinch of flaky salt

Greek yoghurt, to serve

An autumnal dessert with a beautiful contrast of textures and flavours. The batter is made with rice flour to keep it gluten-free, so eat these straight away to retain that light, crisp coating. I like tossing the fried bananas in a cinnamon-sugar-salt combo just for that extra bit of flair. Any leftover caramel can be covered and stored for a few days in the fridge. It goes very well on other desserts in this chapter, too, such as the Mille Crêpe Cake (see page 200).

Start by making the caramel. Put the sugar and 60ml (2fl oz/¼ cup) water in a pan over a medium-low heat. Do not stir, but shake the pan around to get rid of any clumps of sugar as it melts. When the sugar has melted and the caramel has taken on a golden brown colour (this will take 5–7 minutes), add the cream, miso and butter and whisk well until fully combined. You should have a sauce with a smooth, pourable consistency. Set aside.

For the bananas, slice them on an angle in half and then in half again and put in a bowl. The pieces should be around 6cm (2½in) long.

Heat the oil in a large, heavy-based pan over a medium heat. While it's heating up, make the batter by whisking the rice flour with 3½ tablespoons of water in a bowl until smooth, ensuring there are no lumps.

When the oil is hot, working in batches, dip the banana pieces into the batter, then carefully add to the hot oil. Fry for 2–3 minutes on each side, using tongs to turn, until golden all over. Using a slotted spoon, transfer to a draining rack set over a plate to drain the excess oil. Keep warm while you cook the remaining banana pieces.

In a bowl, mix the cinnamon, sugar and salt. Sprinkle the mixture evenly over the bananas while they're still hot.

To serve, dollop the yoghurt onto plates, top with the bananas and serve the caramel sauce on the side.

dango with sweet and salty sauce

mitarashi dango

Makes 20 balls

V + VG

For the mitarashi glaze

3 tbsp white caster (superfine) sugar

1 tbsp soy sauce

4 tbsp water

1 tsp potato starch

For the dango (rice-flour dumplings)

100g (3½oz) shiratamako (sweet rice flour/glutinous rice flour)

125g (4½oz) silken tofu

These are an icon of after-school snacking. You'll find them sold on roadsides by temples, on hiking trails and, of course, at every Japanese *konbini* (convenience shop). I used to frequent the same shop in Tokyo, where the old man serving would grill up perfect soft rice-flour dumplings that were skewered and coated in a sweet, salty, gloopy glaze of sugar and soy sauce. I'd eat as I walked – normally frowned upon in Japanese culture, but these were too good to wait for, as the mitarashi glaze dripped down your hand with every bite. This recipe is my ode to that mitarashi dango, one that you can make in your very own kitchen.

Shiratamako, also known as sweet rice flour or glutinous rice flour, is commonly used to make wagashi (traditional Japanese desserts), most commonly mochi and dango. The flour is chunky and coarse and becomes a pliable dough when mixed with water. It can be bought in Japanese supermarkets or online. Please note that this cannot be substituted with regular rice flour, which has a much coarser texture and will not yield the same results.

Start by making the mitarashi glaze. Put all the ingredients in a small pan over a medium heat and let it come to a simmer. Simmer for 2–3 minutes until thickened and glossy. Set aside.

For the dango, simply mix the shiratamako and tofu in a bowl using your hands until it becomes a fairly stiff dough ball. It's less about kneading here and more about just making sure all the shiratamako is broken up so there are no large clumps. My mum always told me you want it to have the firmness of an earlobe.

Using your hands, roll heaped teaspoons of the dough into about 20 even-sized balls. Bring a large pan of water to the boil. Fill a separate large bowl with ice-cold water. When the water is boiling, add 6–8 dango at a time, making sure not to overfill the pan. After 2–3 minutes, the dango will rise to the surface. Give them an extra 2 minutes, then scoop them out using a slotted spoon and transfer them to the bowl of cold water. Continue cooking the rest in the same way.

When all the balls are cooked, drain them and serve them in bowls with the glaze spooned over, for the easy option. Alternatively, thread 3 dango onto bamboo skewers and sear them slightly on a hot, dry frying pan (skillet) so they get a bit charred on the outside. Glaze with the mitarashi and serve.

DESSERTS

Japanese flan

purin

Serves 4

V

For the caramel topping

50g (1¾oz/¼ cup) white caster (superfine) sugar

For the crème caramel base

200ml (7fl oz/scant 1 cup) whole milk

3½ tbsp single (light) cream

2 medium eggs

40g (1½oz/3¼ tbsp) white caster (superfine) sugar

To serve (optional)

whipped cream

berries of your choice or maraschino cherries

A Japanese staple that's essentially a crème caramel, but a lot lighter and less sweet. Although its roots lie in Portugal, you'll find this in every café, *konbini* (convenience store) and household, and homemade at every grandma's house. The aim is to have a bitter caramel at the top (so cook the sugar that extra minute further than you think you need) on top of a smooth custard that is steamed until it's still wobbly. It feels pretty traditional and homemade to serve it just as it is, but I love a dollop of whipped cream and some berries for a bit of tart flavour contrast. This is a nostalgic dessert that always reminds me of family and is loved by adults and children alike.

First, make the caramel topping. Heat the sugar in a pan over a medium heat for 5–7 minutes. Don't stir as it cooks, but swirl it around the pan to ensure it melts and cooks evenly. When the sugar has taken on a deep golden-brown colour, add 2 tablespoons of cold water and mix well by shaking and turning the pan. Wear an oven glove, as it may spit. Pour the caramel evenly into four ramekins and set aside.

For the base, whisk the milk, cream, eggs and sugar in a bowl until fully incorporated, then pour evenly through a fine-mesh sieve (strainer) into the four ramekins. Pour gently to prevent bubbles from appearing on the surface.

Find a large, lidded pan that's big enough to hold the four ramekins comfortably in a single layer. Pour in enough water to come halfway up the sides of the ramekins, once you're ready to place them in the pan. Set the pan over a high heat and bring the water up to the boil. Meanwhile, tie a clean dish towel around the base of the lid (this will prevent steam from dripping onto the custard as it cooks).

Once the water has boiled, turn the heat to the lowest setting and put the four ramekins in the pan. Put the lid on and set a timer for 12 minutes. When the time is up, turn off the heat, leave the lid on and leave to steam for another 12 minutes.

Wear an oven glove to take the ramekins out of the hot water and let them cool to room temperature, then transfer to the fridge to cool for at least 1 hour.

To serve, carefully upturn the ramekins onto small plates. You might need to first loosen the edges with a knife to help remove them. Serve with the whipped cream and a scattering of berries – or a maraschino cherry if you're feeling extra kitsch.

matcha and white chocolate biscuits

matcha to choco no cookie

Makes 10

V

50g (1¾oz/3½ tbsp) salted butter, softened

45g (1½oz/3½ tbsp) white caster (superfine) sugar

1 egg yolk

120g (4¼oz/1 cup minus 1½ tbsp) flour

2g (1 tsp) matcha powder

50g (1¾oz) white chocolate, broken into rough chunks

Biscuits (cookies) make for great gifting, or just to have at home for your afternoon cup of tea. I love these because they have a great crumb and they're not too sweet. They are also super simple and only require six ingredients. If you're not a fan of matcha (green tea powder), you could easily leave it out. I sometimes use a bit of kinako (roasted soybean powder; see page 212) in these, too.

Combine the butter and sugar in a mixing bowl, using an electric whisk, until fluffy and pale, around 5 minutes. Add the egg yolk and mix well.

Sift in the flour and matcha and fold until well combined, then stir in the white chocolate chunks. Chill the dough in the fridge for 30 minutes.

Preheat the oven to 140°C fan/160°C/325°F/Gas mark 3. Line a baking sheet with baking paper.

Once chilled, use a rolling pin to roll the dough out to a thickness of around 7mm (³/₈in). Cut the dough into 10 circles using a 6cm (2½in) cookie cutter, lay them on the prepared baking sheet and bake for 14 minutes until very lightly browned around the edges.

Let them cool completely before serving.

DESSERTS

roasted sweet potatoes

yaki imo

Serves 4

V

2 Japanese sweet potatoes

1½ tbsp salted butter

vanilla ice cream

flaky salt

A four-ingredient recipe that provides the comfort, warmth and perfect amount of sweetness you crave on a cold winter's night.

The key is to use Japanese sweet potatoes, which are starchier, less watery and more *hoku hoku* (meaning soft, warm, freshly roasted) with a chestnut-like flavour. They have a dark-purple skin and white or yellow flesh. You can buy these from Asian supermarkets, where they might be called beniharuka or beniazuma (for the white or yellow-fleshed ones with a purple or red skin) or look out for marusaki imo for the purple-fleshed ones. I would advise against using regular orange-skinned ones for this, as they're too mushy and watery.

Preheat the oven to 160°C fan/180°C/365°F/Gas mark 4 and pierce the potatoes with a fork.

Once the oven is hot, roast the potatoes on the middle rack for 1 hour–1 hour 10 minutes until you can easily pierce the flesh with a knife. Don't worry if some of the sugary juices seep out as the potatoes cook – this is a good sign.

Once cooked, set aside for 10 minutes, then score the skins so you can break them apart lengthways. Divide among four plates and spread over the butter. Top each with a small scoop of cold vanilla ice cream and a pinch of flaky salt, and eat immediately.

red bean pancakes

dorayaki

Makes 10

V

For the pancakes

3 medium eggs

100g (3½oz/½ cup) white caster (superfine) sugar

1 tbsp honey

1 tbsp mirin

180g (6½oz/1⅓ cups) plain (all-purpose) flour

1 tsp bicarbonate of soda (baking soda)

pinch of salt

1 tsp neutral oil, such as rapeseed (canola) or sunflower

For the filling

200ml (7fl oz/scant 1 cup) cream, whipped to soft peaks

250g (9oz) anko (sweet red bean paste)

An icon of Japanese *oyatsu* (afternoon snack), these pancakes are sweetened with sugar and honey and are, surprisingly, dairy-free. I love filling them with anko (sweet red bean paste), which is very traditional. Anko plays a huge role in Japanese sweet culture. It's made of adzuki beans that are simmered until soft and sweetened with sugar, and is often used as a stuffing in sweet treats such as manju (steamed buns with red bean) and daifuku (mochi with red bean). You can buy readymade anko in cans for easy use (what I normally use) or buy adzuki beans and simmer them at home yourself. In my household, we also like to load these up with whipped cream, or eat them filled with a slab of cold salted butter and a pinch of flaky salt for the perfect combination of sweet and salty.

Keep a vigilant eye on these as they cook, to make sure they don't burn – it can happen in the blink of an eye, even at a low heat.

In a mixing bowl, whisk the eggs, sugar, honey, mirin and 3½ tablespoons of water for 2 minutes, or until the mixture is starting to turn paler. Sift in the flour, bicarbonate of soda and salt, mix to combine, then set the batter aside to rest for 1 hour.

After this time, add another 3½ tablespoons of water to the batter and mix gently until completely incorporated. The batter should have the familiar consistency of pancake batter.

Heat a non-stick frying pan (skillet) over a medium heat, add the oil, then wipe off the excess with a paper towel. Drop 1 tablespoon of batter from a height of about 20cm (8in) onto the pan; the pancakes should spread out to about 10cm (4in) in diameter. Turn the heat to low and cook for 1 minute on one side, then carefully flip and cook for 40 seconds on the other. Cook one or two pancakes at a time, being careful to keep a close eye on them. You will have enough batter for 20 pancakes. As they are cooked, transfer the pancakes to a plate, keep warm and cover with a damp dish towel while you cook the others.

Once all are cooked, get two pancakes ready to sandwich together. Spread one pancake with whipped cream and the other with anko, then sandwich them together. (Do not overfill them, as the filling will explode out the edges when you eat them.) Continue filling the remaining pancakes. Wrap each pancake sandwich in cling film (plastic wrap) and let them set (at room temperature or in the fridge) for at least 30 minutes before serving.

sesame mochi

goma to kinako no mochi

Serves 2

V + VG

2 tbsp ground black sesame seeds

1½ tbsp toasted black sesame seeds

1 tbsp kinako (roasted soybean flour)

1 tbsp white caster (superfine) sugar

pinch of salt

2 kirimochi (see page 18)

1 tbsp shibazuke (pickled aubergine/eggplant), to serve (optional)

These are ideal for those who want a little something at the end of dinner that isn't too sweet. I came across these on a freezing February day at a tiny old shop called Amasake Tea House in the town of Hakone. We were cold and it was so rainy outside that the only thing that could possibly warm us up would be a hot hojicha (roasted green tea) and sweet, squidgy mochi. The mochi was boiled in water on top of a stove used to heat the whole room and was then coated in a powder I'd never tried before. The sesame coating was the perfect balance of sweet, nutty and slightly salty. It was served with a side of tsukemono (pickled or preserved vegetables) that worked so well together. The topping is incredibly easy to make and any leftovers would be delicious sprinkled on top of thick Greek yoghurt with honey. The method below is the best way to boil mochi, which my mum taught me a long time ago. It's absolutely foolproof and you'll get melty, soft and delicious mochi every time.

Kinako is roasted soybean powder that's commonly used in traditional Japanese desserts. It's finely ground and you can sweeten it by adding sugar. You'll find it in Japanese supermarkets, as well as bags of kirimochi (dried mochi rectangles) and shibazuke (pickled aubergines/eggplant) or other tsukemono that you might like.

Put the ground sesame seeds, toasted sesame seeds, kinako, sugar and salt in a shallow bowl. Mix and set aside.

Put the kirimochi in a pan of cold water set over a high heat. Bring to the boil, then reduce the heat to low and let cook for 2 minutes. You'll have perfectly cooked, soft mochi every time.

Once the mochi are cooked, dust in the sesame mixture, making sure they are fully coated. Serve while still hot, with the shibazuke on the side.

DESSERTS

the sweet treat　ちょっとした甘い物

What you need to know about Japanese desserts is that they tick all the boxes – and they're in a totally different world to that of European and American pastries and cake. Texturally, they've got it all: crunchy, chewy, soft. On top of that there's variety in temperature, from ice-cold kakigori (sweetened shaved ice) to warming zenzai (a sweet red-bean soup). They've got the right balance of sweet but not too sweet, which is the highest compliment a Japanese person could probably give to a dessert – and they're ideal enjoyed alongside a coffee or strong matcha (green tea). Let me introduce you to a few of note.

Anmitsu　餡蜜
A traditional Japanese dessert combining ingredients with a variety of textures and flavours. You really need to look at it in detail. The base is normally made up of kanten, a flavourless jelly made from algae, which provides a light 'puri puri' texture. The toppings are where it gets exciting, normally consisting of anko (sweet red bean paste), shiratama (glutinous rice flour balls), ice cream of some sort (usually vanilla or chocolate) and a variety of seasonal fruits. The whole thing is topped with endomame, a type of pea that's boiled and chilled.

The final kick of sweetness comes from kuromitsu: a rich, dark sugar syrup that is made from kokuto, a type of brown sugar from Okinawa, which provides a silky sweetness with a hint of burnt sugar caramel.

Dango　団子
There are countless variations of dango (rice-flour dumplings) and you'll always find them at festivals or outside temples, where they're often grilled on an open fire. The two top flavours you'll see wherever you go are anko (see picture opposite) and mitarashi (see page 204). Anko is soft, chewy dango topped with a thick spread of sweet red bean paste, a simple and very nostalgic dessert for many. Mitarashi dango are what I see as Japan's version of salted caramel – a sweet and savoury caramel is made with soy sauce and sugar and used to coat the dango for an addictive treat.

Kakigori　かき氷
A summer dessert made from shaved ice that's loved by children and adults alike. There's something so nostalgic about going to *natsumatsuri* (summer festivals) in the sweltering humidity of summer and getting a bowl of shaved ice topped with sweet syrups. Commonly, you'll find the ice topped with condensed milk and a variety of fruit syrups. This is one to be eaten quickly, coming hand-in-hand with brain freeze, naturally.

THE SWEET TREAT

Sakura mochi 桜餅
For lovers of savoury and sweet in a dessert, this will be right up your street. Traditionally served for *Hanamatsuri* (Girl's Day, 3 March), this is a springtime treat. The exterior, made from glutinous rice, is nicely chewy, and the sweet red-bean filling is lightly crushed. It's covered in a blanket of salt-pickled *sakura* leaf (young leaves from a cherry tree) and sometimes salt-pickled cherry blossoms are used for decoration.

Soufflé cheesecake
スフレーチーズケーキ
Cheesecakes are objectively good wherever you go: creamy, strangely light – even though you're essentially eating a tub of cream cheese – and delicious. Japanese chefs combined the whipped egg whites from a soufflé with the traditional baked cheesecake to create, well, a soufflé cheesecake. Much lighter than the original, it melts in your mouth upon the first bite and has a creamy texture. It's a lot less sweet and has more of a tang than you'd expect from a dessert, but that's what keeps you going in for more.

Taiyaki たい焼き
A waffle is grilled in a fish-shaped, cast-iron pan and filled with plenty of exciting flavours, from anko (sweet red bean paste) to custard. Whatever the season, you'll find vendors all over Japan selling these, from a little hole in the wall or travelling the streets with a handcart. The outside is crunchy in places and the light waffle shell is filled with warmth and sweetness, making it the ideal street snack, especially for the autumn months.

Zenzai 善哉
A sweet bean soup may not be the first thing that comes to mind when you think of desserts, but there's something so comforting about adzuki beans that have been slowly simmering and are lightly sweetened. The soup is topped with a grilled kirimochi (glutinous rice cake; see page 18), creating the perfect harmony of crunchy and chewy on top of soft and mellow.

Japanese baking　日本のパン屋さん

Creative and ingenious, Japanese baking deserves to be better known around the world. Japanese bakers are skilled at creating the fluffiest, lightest, slightly sweet breads, and are continually creating new things you simply can't get anywhere else. A first-time visitor might be surprised that Japan has such a vast variety of breads. By 'breads' you might be thinking of the buttery croissants, viennoiserie and baguettes you find in French bakeries, or you might even be thinking of sausage rolls, steak bakes and doughnuts. Japan has it all and offers a whole new world of fusion and excitement. The catch-all name for bread is 'pan' in Japanese, derived from the Portuguese word 'pao' – the Portuguese introduced bread-baking to Japan in the 16th century. Many of the baked creations are made and eaten across the whole country, but often with a local twist.

What really started the bread trend in Japan is shokupan, a milk bread with a soft texture that pulls apart when you cut into it and a buttery, sweet (but not too sweet flavour). The popularity of shokupan rose after the Second World War when there was a rice shortage and wheat became more readily available. Now, don't even try to compare this to your bog-standard white loaf; it's so much more. A lot of Japanese rolls are based on this bread, so you'll probably have shokupan encasing your egg mayo or the fruit sandwiches (just sliced bread, fresh fruit and whipped cream) that are so popular in Japan.

On the following pages is a list of some of the most popular items you're likely to find in a Japanese bakery. Among them are a bread stuffed with curry that's deep-fried until piping hot; doughnuts made with rice flour so they have a 'mochi-mochi' chewy texture; sweet red bean rolls with a thick slab of salty butter . . . and that's only the beginning. A world of Japanese breads awaits.

A butter roll　あんバターロール
A simple white roll is filled with lightly mashed anko (sweet red bean paste; see page 211), providing creaminess and a bit of texture. For those wanting to take it to the next level, you'll normally find the option of a slice of cold, salty butter in there: a proper slice, not a measly spread, as you want to see bite marks in it, so there are clearly defined layers of the golden-brown roll, the yellow slab of butter and the burgundy adzuki beans.

Chikuwa pan　ちくわパン
A long, buttery bun is sliced open and stuffed with isobeage (fried chikuwa fishcakes; see page 181), finely sliced cabbage, mayo and bites of bright-pink benishoga (pickled ginger). Chikuwa pan is something of a mystery to me – it manages to recreate the flavour of okonomiyaki in a bread. Every bite is a surprise of soft, crunchy, tart and creamy.

Gobo sarada pan　牛蒡サラダパン
This roll is filled with a root vegetable called gobo (burdock root), which is boiled or sautéed and mixed with carrots and mayonnaise to create a slightly crunchy – and very delicious – filling for soft bread. This is one for those who love mayo-based salads, and is a step up from potato salad.

Hot dog　ホットドッグ
Japanese hot dogs have a memorable texture: the skin snaps as you bite into it, and you're welcomed with a nicely juicy sausage. It's covered in ketchup and mustard and baked in a roll and – if you're lucky – you'll find a sprinkling of gooey melted cheese on there too.

Kare pan　カレーパン
Picture this: piping hot, savoury, crispy, fluffy, oozy goodness. That's kare pan for you. A soft dough is filled with a thick Japanese curry (chicken, vegetables, tender beef, spicy minced/ground lamb) and coated in panko breadcrumbs before being deep-fried. The unmissable result is a must-have when visiting any Japanese bakery (and it's a good excuse to try them all, because each shop's version is slightly different). A memory that stands out in my mind is going to Karepan Kenkyujo in the city of Hiroshima for their unbelievable bread selection – but mainly the daily variations of kare pan: beef curry, tomato curry in a sun-dried tomato bread, original spicy curry . . . One for the books.

Korokke pan　コロッケパン
A potato or vegetable croquette stuffed into bread – this is the ultimate sandwich. Think chip butty (a french-fry sandwich) but levelled up by ten. Of course, you've got to slather it in okonomiyaki sauce (see page 22) for the full experience, so it's dripping with each bite. You can never go amiss with this family favourite, which is also great for vegetarians.

Melon pan メロンパン
You've probably realized by now that the base of most Japanese bread is deliciously buttery, soft and light. Melon pan is an honourable exception. The name has nothing to do with the flavour but is given for its appearance: the crunchy hatched shell around the top of the bread resembles a melon. It's crunchy and sweet and sometimes you'll find it filled with whipped cream for an extra-special after-school snack.

Mentaiko pan 明太子パン
A French baguette style of bread that's crunchy on the outside and airy on the inside is sliced open and spread with mentaiko butter – salty fish eggs mixed into butter (see page 18). It's toasted again to create a double crunch and for the super-savoury butter to really soak in. Eating a good mentaiko pan fresh out the oven is somewhat of an other-worldly experience.

Nejiri pan 捻りパン
Doughnut lovers, take note. This is the lightest and airiest doughnut that you could easily eat ten of. *Nejiri*, meaning 'twisted', is a dough that is deep-fried and coated in caster (superfine) sugar. They're nothing fancy, but there's not much better than a hot doughnut that comes in a bag of crunchy sugar.

Toumorokoshi mayo pan
とうもろこしパン
A light brioche-like dough topped with (or sometimes kneaded into) sweet kernels of corn and a drizzle of mayonnaise. Baking the mayo gives it an almost cheese-like effect that adds a punch of creaminess to every sweet bite. There's something so simple but so effective about this bread. A summertime special.

where to buy Japanese ingredients

UK

- **Japan Centre:** 35b Panton St, London, SW1Y 4EA, United Kingdom
japancentre.com

- **Longdan Oriental Supermarket:** 23 Parkway, London, NW1 7PG, United Kingdom
longdan.co.uk

- **H Mart:** Unit 1 Leigh Cl, New Malden, KT3 3NW, United Kingdom
hmart.co.uk

- **Whole Foods:** 63-97 Kensington High St, London, W8 5SE, United Kingdom
wholefoodsmarket.co.uk

- **See Woo:** 18-20 Lisle St, London, WC2H 7BA, United Kingdom
seewoouk.com

- **Thai Smile:** 283–285 King St, London, W6 9NH, United Kingdom
www.thaismile.com/shop/

- **Yukata** (online): shop.yutaka.london

- **Waso** (online): waso.tokyo

US: online and nationwide

- **Hanamaru:** hanamarumart.us

- **Gohan Market:** gohanmarket.com

- **Whole Foods Market**

- **Trader Joe's**

- **Amazon**

West Coast

- **Marukai Market** (multiple locations): 123 S Onizuka St. #105, Los Angeles, CA 90012, United States
marukai.com/pages/little-tokyo

- **Mitsuwa** (multiple locations): 3760 S Centinela Ave, Los Angeles, CA 90066, United States
mitsuwa.com

- **Nijiya** (multiple locations): 2130 Sawtelle Blvd # 105, Los Angeles, CA 90025, United States
nijiya.com

- **Seiwa Market:** 21815 Hawthorne Blvd, Torrance, CA 90503, United States
seiwamarket.com

East Coast

- **Sunrise Mart:** 494 Broome St, New York, NY 10013, United States
sunrisemart.com

- **Katagiri Japanese Grocery:** 370 Lexington Ave, New York, NY 10017, United States
katagiri.com/collections

- **Dainobu:** 36 W 56th St, New York, NY 10019, United States
dainobunyc.com

- **Midoriya:** 167 N 9th St, Brooklyn, NY 11211, United States

- **Yamada:** 450 6th Ave, New York, NY 10011, United States

WHERE TO BUY JAPANESE INGREDIENTS

223

menu suggestions

quick and easy

For when you're short on time, but still want something delicious

- Oyakodon (chicken and egg rice bowl; see page 35)
- Zuke Maguro Don (marinated tuna rice bowl; see page 40)
- Yaki Mochi (grilled mochi; see page 56)
- Saba Tama Udon (smoked mackerel and egg udon; see page 74)
- Gyuudon (beef and onion rice bowl; see page 80)
- Ebi Chilli (sweet and sour prawns; see page 100)
- Taco Rice (Okinawan taco rice; see page 128)
- Mentaiko Pasta (spaghetti with spicy cod's roe; see page 43)
- Onigiri (rice balls; see page 64)
- Kyuri to Ume no Salada (cucumber umeboshi salad; see page 169)
- Salmon no Foil Yaki (salmon grilled in foil; see page 99)
- Goma to Kinako no Mochi (sesame mochi; see page 212)

veggie favourites

Veg-forward plates that deliver on flavour

- Tomato no Marine no Somen (marinated tomato somen; see page 53)
- Tendon (tempura rice bowl; see page 105)
- Yasai Korokke (vegetable croquettes; see page 109)
- Dashimaki Tamago (rolled egg omelette; see page 194)
- Kitsune Udon (simmered fried-tofu udon; see page 44)
- Kabocha Soup (pumpkin soup; see page 47)

cooking to impress

Showstopping ingredients and masterful techniques

- Steak Don (steak rice bowl; see page 127)//
- Hotate no Butter Shoyu Yaki (butter and soy sauce scallops; see page 161)
- Tai no Sashimi (sea bream sashimi; see page 162)
- Hotate to Ichigo no Carpaccio (scallop carpaccio with strawberries; see page 174)
- Tori Katsu Sando (chicken katsu sandwich; see page 67) or Nasu Katsu Sando (aubergine/eggplant katsu sandwich; see page 73)
- Harumaki (Japanese spring rolls; see page 115)
- Kani Cream Korokke (crab cream croquettes; see page 142)
- Mille Crêpe Cake (layered crêpe cake; see page 200)

home izakaya

Snacks and sharers for feasting with friends

- Tori no Gomae (chicken cups with sesame dressing; see page 36)
- Buta Maki (pork katsu rolls; see page 131)
- Gyoza (pan-fried dumplings; see pages 138–41) or Sui Gyoza (boiled dumplings; see page 143)
- Kani Cream Korokke (crab cream croquettes; see page 142)
- Karaage (Japanese fried chicken; see page 149)
- Kimchi to Maguro no Otsumami (kimchi and tuna otsumami; see page 170)
- Potato Salada (the ultimate potato salad; see page 178)
- Kyuri to Shio Kombu Salada (cucumber and shio kombu salad; see page 185)
- Toumorokoshi Tempura (corn tempura; see page 189)

index

aburaage (fried tofu pockets) 44
agedashi nasu (dashi-marinated aubergines) 182
ajitsuke tamago (marinated eggs) 186
amakara tebasaki (sweet-and-salty chicken wings) 166
anko (sweet red bean paste): red bean pancakes 211
'anything goes' nabe 124
asari no sake mushi (sake-steamed clams) 153
aubergines (eggplants):
    aubergine katsu sandwich 73
    dashi-marinated aubergines 182
    mabo aubergine 96
    sea bream sashimi 162
    tempura rice bowl 105

bamboo shoots: Japanese spring rolls 115
beef: beef and onion rice bowl 80
    curry udon 87
    Japanese beef hotpot 83
    meat and potato stew 104
    steak rice bowl 127
    stewed burgers 88
bell peppers *see* capsicums
biscuits, matcha and white chocolate 208
blenders/whisks 27
bread: chicken katsu sandwich 67
    see also panko breadcrumbs
burgers: chicken and tofu burgers 91
    stewed burgers 88
buta maki (pork katsu rolls) 131
buta no kakuni (braised pork belly) 154
buta to enoki maki (enoki mushrooms wrapped in pork belly) 95
butabara and atsuage (pork belly with thick fried tofu) 177
butter and soy sauce scallops 161

cabbage: 'anything goes' nabe 124
    Japanese savoury pancake 110
    meat and cabbage croquettes 146
    pan-fried dumplings 138–41
    slaw 73

cake, layered crêpe 200
capers: tartare sauce 114
capsicums (bell peppers):
    crispy tofu rice bowl with pork 48
    egg omelette rice 118
    meat-stuffed peppers 123
    tempura rice bowl 105
caramel: fried banana with miso caramel 203
    Japanese flan 207
carpaccio: scallop carpaccio 174
carrots: katsu curry 84
    meat and potato stew 104
    vegetable croquettes 109
cheese: cod's roe and potato harumaki 193
    flat gyoza with chicken and cheese 190
    grilled mochi 56
    grilled rice balls 66
    ham and cheese katsu 157
chicken: boiled dumplings 143
    chicken and egg rice bowl 35
    chicken and lotus root pasta 63
    chicken and tofu burgers 91
    chicken cups with sesame dressing 36
    chicken katsu sandwich 67
    chicken meatballs 150
    chicken-stuffed lotus root 121
    chicken thighs with ponzu sauce 173
    cold chilli-oil soba noodles 52
    egg omelette rice 118
    flat gyoza with chicken and cheese 190
    ground chicken and egg rice bowl 103
    Japanese fried chicken 149
    marinated fried chicken 92
    stir-fried chicken with radishes 176
    sweet-and-salty chicken wings 166
    western-style cream stew 120
chikuwa: fried fishcakes 181
chocolate: matcha and white chocolate biscuits 208
chopsticks 27
cinnamon: fried banana with miso caramel 203
clams, sake-steamed 153
cod's roe: cod's roe and potato harumaki 193

spaghetti with spicy cod's roe 43
corn tempura 189
cornichons: tartare sauce 114
crab cream croquettes 142
cream: layered crêpe cake 200
　red bean pancakes 211
cream stew (western-style cream stew) 120
crème caramel: Japanese flan 207
croquettes: crab cream croquettes 142
　meat and cabbage croquettes 146
　vegetable croquettes 109
cucumber: chicken cups with sesame dressing 36
　cucumber and shio kombu salad 185
　cucumber umeboshi salad 169
　slaw 73
　the ultimate potato salad 178
curry 16
　curry udon 87
　katsu curry 84

dango with sweet and salty sauce 204
dashi 15
　'anything goes' nabe 124
　chicken and egg rice bowl 35
　curry udon 87
　prawn and dashi pasta 60
　simmered fried-tofu udon 44
dashimaki tamago (rolled egg omelette) 194
dipping sauce 52, 91, 109
dorayaki (red bean pancakes) 211
dumplings: boiled dumplings 143
　dango with sweet and salty sauce 204
　pan-fried dumplings 138–41

ebi to dashi no pasta (prawn and dashi pasta) 60
ebi chilli (sweet and sour prawns) 100
eggplants *see* aubergines
eggs: braised pork belly 154
　chicken and egg rice bowl 35
　cold ramen 39
　dipping sauce 52
　egg omelette rice 118
　ground chicken and egg rice bowl 103

marinated eggs 186
marinated tuna rice bowl 40
rolled egg omelette 194
tartare sauce 92, 114
tempura rice bowl 105
enoki mushrooms wrapped in pork belly 95
equipment 27

fishcakes, fried 181
flavours 15
fried banana with miso caramel 203

gohan 30
goma to kinako no mochi (sesame mochi) 212
graters 27
gyoza wrappers: boiled dumplings 143
　flat gyoza with chicken and cheese 190
　gyoza (pan-fried dumplings) 138–41
gyuudon (beef and onion rice bowl) 80

ham: cold ramen 39
　ham and cheese katsu 157
　the ultimate potato salad 178
ham to cheese no katsu (ham and cheese katsu) 157
harumaki (Japanese spring rolls) 115
　cod's roe and potato harumaki 193
hiyashi chuka (cold ramen) 39
hiyashi rayu soba (cold chilli-oil soba noodles) 52
hondashi (stock) 16
　prawn and dashi pasta 60
hotate no butter shoyu yaki (butter and soy sauce scallops) 161
hotate to ichigo no carpaccio (scallop carpaccio with strawberries) 174
hotpots: 'anything goes' nabe 124
　Japanese beef hotpot 83

ingredients 16–24
isobeage (fried fishcakes) 181

Japanese beef hotpot 83
Japanese flan 207
Japanese savoury pancake 110

Japanese spring rolls 115
kabocha squash: kabocha (pumpkin) soup 47
   tempura rice bowl 105
   western-style cream stew 120
kani cream korokke (crab cream croquettes) 142
karaage (Japanese fried chicken) 149
kare udon (curry udon) 87
katsu: ham and cheese katsu 157
   pork katsu rolls 131
katsu kare (katsu curry) 84
Kewpie mayonnaise 18
khaki furai (fried oysters) 114
kimchi to maguro no otsumami (kimchi and tuna otsumami) 170
kinoko takikomi gohan (mixed mushroom rice) 112
kirimochi (rice cakes) 18
   grilled mochi 56
   kirimochi: sesame mochi 212
kitsune udon (simmered fried-tofu udon) 44
knives 27
kyuri to shio kombi salada (cucumber and shio kombu salad) 185
kyuri to ume no salada (cucumber umeboshi salad) 169

leeks: 'anything goes' nabe 124
   braised pork belly 154
    Japanese beef hotpot 83
    simmered fried-tofu udon 44
lettuce: chicken cups with sesame dressing 36
linguine: prawn and dashi pasta 60
lotus root: chicken and lotus root pasta 63
   chicken-stuffed lotus root 121

mabo nasu (mabo aubergine) 96
mackerel *see* smoked mackerel
   maguro no tataki (grilled tuna steak) 158
matcha and white chocolate biscuits 208
mayonnaise 18
   roasted sesame dressing 36
   slaw 73
   tartare sauce 92, 114
   the ultimate potato salad 178
meat and cabbage croquettes 146
meat and potato stew 104
meat-stuffed peppers 123
meatballs, chicken 150
menchi katsu (meat and cabbage croquettes) 146
mentaiko (pollock roe) 18
mentaiko pasta (spaghetti with spicy cod's roe) 43
mentsuyu 18
   dipping sauce 52
milk: Japanese flan 207
mille crêpe cake (layered crêpe cake) 200
mirin 15, 18
   marinated eggs 186
miso 21
   fried banana with miso caramel 203
   miso shiru (miso soup) 28, 31
mitarashi dango (dango with sweet and salty sauce) 204
mochi (rice cakes): grilled mochi 56
   sesame mochi 212
mushrooms: chicken and lotus root pasta 63
   egg omelette rice 118
   enoki mushrooms wrapped in pork belly 95
   katsu curry 84
   mixed mushroom rice 112
   Okinawan taco rice 128
   salmon grilled in foil 99
   stewed burgers 88
   tempura rice bowl 105

nagaimo (Chinese mountain yam): Japanese savoury pancake 110
nandemo nabe 'anything goes' nabe 124
nasu katsu sando (aubergine katsu sandwich) 73
nentaiko to potato no harumaki (cod's roe and potato harumaki) 193

nikomi hamburg (stewed burgers) 88
nikujaga (meat and potato stew) 104
nikuzume peeman (meat-stuffed peppers) 123
noodles 21, 76–7
   cold chilli-oil soba noodles 52
   curry udon 87
   Japanese beef hotpot 83
   Japanese spring rolls 115
   marinated tomato somen 53
   meat and potato stew 104
   simmered fried-tofu udon 44
   smoked mackerel and egg udon 74
nori: kimchi and tuna otsumami 170
   rice balls 64

octopus: octopus and tomato pasta 59
   octopus sashimi 165
oils 24
Okinawan taco rice 128
okonomiyaki (Japanese savoury pancake) 110
okonomiyaki sauce 22
okra: fried fishcakes 181
omelettes: egg omelette rice 118
   rolled egg omelette 194
omurice (egg omelette rice) 118
onigiri (rice balls) 64
onions: beef and onion rice bowl 80
   meat and potato stew 104
   tempura rice bowl 105
ovens 27
oyakodon (chicken and egg rice bowl) 35
oysters, fried 114

pancakes: Japanese savoury pancake 110
   red bean pancakes 211
panko breadcrumbs 22
   aubergine katsu sandwich 73
   crab cream croquettes 142
   fried oysters 114
   ham and cheese katsu 157
   katsu curry 84
   meat-stuffed peppers 123
   pork katsu rolls 131
pasta: chicken and lotus root pasta 63

octopus and tomato pasta 59
prawn and dashi pasta 60
spaghetti with spicy cod's roe 43
peppers (bell) *see* capsicums
pickles 15
ponzu sauce 22
   chicken thighs with ponzu sauce 173
pork: 'anything goes' nabe 124
   braised pork belly 154
   crispy tofu rice bowl with pork 48
   curry udon 87
   enoki mushrooms wrapped in pork belly 95
   Japanese savoury pancake 110
   Japanese spring rolls 115
   katsu curry 84
   mabo aubergine 96
   meat and cabbage croquettes 146
   meat-stuffed peppers 123
   Okinawan taco rice 128
   pan-fried dumplings 138B41
   pork belly with thick fried tofu 177
   pork katsu rolls 131
   stewed burgers 88
potato salada (the ultimate potato salad) 178
potatoes: cod's roe and potato harumaki 193
   katsu curry 84
   meat and potato stew 104
   the ultimate potato salad 178
   vegetable croquettes 109
   western-style cream stew 120
prawns: prawn and dashi pasta 60
   sweet and sour prawns 100
pumpkin soup 47
purin (Japanese flan) 207

radishes: scallop carpaccio with strawberries 174
   stir-fried chicken with radishes 176
ramen noodles 21
   cold ramen 39
red bean pancakes 211
rice 22, 28
   beef and onion rice bowl 80
   crispy tofu rice bowl with pork 48

INDEX

egg omelette rice 118
gohan 30
grilled rice balls 66
ground chicken and egg rice bowl 103
marinated tuna rice bowl 40
mixed mushroom rice 112
Okinawan taco rice 128
rice balls 64
steak rice bowl 127
rice vinegar 22

saba tama udon (smoked mackerel and egg udon) 74
sake 15, 23
   marinated eggs 186
   sake-steamed clams 153
salads: cucumber and shio kombu salad 185
   cucumber umeboshi salad 169
   the ultimate potato salad 178
   salmon no foil yaki (salmon grilled in foil) 99
salt 15, 24
sandwiches: aubergine katsu sandwich 73
   chicken katsu sandwich 67
sashimi: octopus sashimi 165
   sea bream sashimi 162
sauces: dipping sauce 52, 91, 109
   ponzu sauce 173
   tartare sauce 92, 114
savoury flavours 15
scallops: butter and soy sauce scallops 161
   scallop carpaccio with strawberries 174
sea bream sashimi 162
seaweed 23
sesame seeds 22
   roasted sesame dressing 36
   sesame mochi 212
shichimi togarashi (spice blend) 23
shio kombu (kelp) 23
   cucumber and shio kombu salad 185
shoyu (soy sauce) 24
slaw 73
smoked mackerel and egg udon 74
soba noodles 21

cold chilli-oil soba noodles 52
soborodon (ground chicken and egg rice bowl) 103
somen noodles 21
   marinated tomato somen 53
soups: miso soup 28, 31
   pumpkin soup 47
soy sauce 15
   butter and soy sauce scallops 161
   marinated eggs 186
spaghetti: octopus and tomato pasta 59
   spaghetti with spicy cod's roe 43
spinach: boiled dumplings 143
   simmered fried-tofu udon 44
spring roll wrappers: cod's roe and potato harumaki 193
   Japanese spring rolls 115
squash: pumpkin soup 47
   tempura rice bowl 105
   western-style cream stew 120
steak don (steak rice bowl) 127
stews: 'anything goes' nabe 124
   Japanese beef hotpot 83
   meat and potato stew 104
   western-style cream stew 120
stock 16
strawberries: layered crêpe cake 200
   scallop carpaccio with strawberries 174
sugar 15, 24
sui gyoza (boiled dumplings) 143
sukiyaki (Japanese beef hotpot) 83
sweet-and-salty chicken wings 166
sweet flavours 15
sweet potatoes, roasted 210
sweetcorn: corn tempura 189
   the ultimate potato salad 178
   vegetable croquettes 109
sweet and sour prawns 100

taco rice (Okinawan taco rice) 128
taco to ponzu no sashimi (octopus sashimi) 165
taco to tomato no pasta (octopus and tomato pasta) 59
tagliatelle: chicken and lotus root pasta 63
tai no sashimi (sea bream sashimi) 162

tartare sauce 92, 114
tempura: corn tempura 189
  tempura rice bowl 105
tendon (tempura rice bowl) 105
tofu: 'anything goes' nabe 124
  chicken and tofu burgers 91
  crispy tofu rice bowl with pork 48
  dango with sweet and salty sauce 204
  Japanese beef hotpot 83
  miso soup 31
  pork belly with thick fried tofu 177
  simmered fried-tofu udon 44
tofu to buta no itame (crispy tofu rice bowl with pork) 48
tomato no marine no somen (marinated tomato somen) 53
tomatoes: grilled tuna steak 158
  marinated tomato somen 53
  octopus and tomato pasta 59
  prawn and dashi pasta 60
  stewed burgers 88
tools 27
tori hamburg (chicken and tofu burgers) 91
tori katsu sando (chicken katsu sandwich) 67
tori momo no ponzu sauce (chicken thighs with ponzu sauce) 173
tori nanban (marinated fried chicken) 92
tori no gomae (chicken cups with sesame dressing) 36
tori to cheese no gyoza (flat gyoza with chicken and cheese) 190
tori to kabu no itame (stir-fried chicken with radishes) 176
tori to renkon no pasta (chicken and lotus root pasta) 63
torizume renkon (chicken-stuffed lotus root) 121
toumorokoshi tempura (corn tempura) 189
tsukune (chicken meatballs) 150
tuna: grilled tuna steak 158
  kimchi and tuna otsumami 170
  marinated tuna rice bowl 40

udon noodles 21
  curry udon 87
  simmered fried-tofu udon 44
  smoked mackerel and egg udon 74
the ultimate potato salad 178
umeboshi plums 24
  cucumber umeboshi salad 169
  pork katsu rolls 131

vegetable croquettes 109
vinegar 15, 22

western-style cream stew 120

yaki imo (roasted sweet potatoes) 210
yaki mochi (grilled mochi) 56
yaki onigiri (grilled rice balls) 66
yasai korokke (vegetable croquettes) 109

zuke maguro don (marinated tuna rice bowl) 40

vegetarian/vegan index

'anything goes' nabe (VO/VGO) 124
aubergine katsu sandwich (V/VGO) 73

bananas with miso caramel, fried (V) 203

chicken and egg rice bowl (VO) 35
cod's roe and potato harumaki (VO) 193
cold ramen (VO) 39
corn tempura (V/VG) 189
cucumber and shio kombu salad (V/VG) 185
cucumber umeboshi salad (V/VG) 169
curry udon (VO) 87

dango with sweet and salty sauce (V/VG) 204
dashi-marinated aubergines (VO/VGO) 182

grilled rice balls (V/VGO) 66

Japanese flan (V) 207

katsu curry (VO) 84

layered crêpe cake (V) 200

mabo aubergine (VO/VGO) 96
marinated tomato somen (V/VG) 53
matcha and white chocolate biscuits (V) 208
miso soup (VO/VGO) 31
mixed mushroom rice (V/VG) 112

pumpkin soup (V/VGO) 47

red bean pancakes (V) 211

rice balls (VO/VGO) 64
rolled egg omelette (V) 194

sesame mochi (V/VG) 212
simmered fried-tofu udon (V/VG) 44
steamed rice (V/VG) 30
sweet potatoes, roasted (V) 210

tempura rice bowl (V) 105

key

V – vegetarian
VO – vegetarian option
VG – vegan
VGO – vegan option

essay index

vegetable croquettes (V) 109
anmitsu (dessert) 214

baking 217–19
bread 217–19
butter rolls 218

cheesecake, soufflé 216
chikara udon (noodles with rice cakes) 77
chikuwa pan (stuffed bun) 218

dango (rice-flour dumplings) 214
desserts 214–17

gobo sarada pan (gobo-filled roll) 218
gyoza (pan-dried dumplings) 196
gyusuji nikomi (slow-simmered beef) 196

hamburg 132
hot dogs 218

Japanese baking 217

izakaya 135
izakaya, the 196–7

kake udon (noodles in broth) 76
kakigori (shaved ice dessert) 214
karaage (fried chicken) 132, 196
kare pan (dough stuffed with curry) 218
kare rice (curry rice) 132
kare udon (curry noodles) 77
kawa (skewered chicken skin) 197
kitsune udon (tofu with noodles) 77
korokke pan (vegetable croquette in bread) 218

love letter to Maisen, a 70
lunch noodle, the 76–7

Maisen, Tokyo 70–1
melon pan (bread) 219
mentaiko pan (bread with mentaiko butter) 219

nankotsu (grilled chicken cartilage) 197
negima (chicken thigh with leeks) 197
negitoro (tuna with spring onions) 197
nejiri pan (doughnuts) 219
niku udon (beef and onions) 77
noodles 76–7

otsukemono (pickled vegetables) 197

potato salad 197

restaurants: izakaya 135, 196–7
  Maisen, Tokyo 70–1
  standing restaurants 76
  teishokuya 132–3

sakana teishoku (grilled fish) 133
sakura mochi (dessert) 216
shyogayaki (pork stir-fry) 133
soufflé cheesecake 216
standing restaurants 76
sweet treat, the 214

tachigui (standing restaurants) 76
taiyaki (waffles) 216
tanuki udon (tempura udon) 77
tebasaki (butterflied chicken wing) 197
teishokuya, the 132–3
tempura 133
tempura udon 76
tonkatsu (deep-fried pork) 70–1, 133
toumorokoshi mayo pan (bread with sweetcorn and mayonnaise) 219
tsukune (chicken meatball) 197

wakame udon (noodles with seaweed) 77

yakitori (chicken skewers) 197

zenzai (sweet bean soup) 216

acknowledgements

Who knew writing a cookbook could take such a team, eh? It's actually a bit unbelievable to think about the amount of people involved in a project – from those who commissioned the book, shot it and styled it, to everyone who ate recipes (the town of Yokosuka was most definitely well fed for the year), supported from the other side of the world. It feels like it would take a whole dissertation to thank every single person, as it really does take a village (or in my case, two cities) to raise a child (and in my case, a book).

Thank you to my mum, Midori, for the constant inspiration every single day. For cooking delicious food for me since the day I was born and putting your heart and soul into everything. You're the creativity that runs through my veins and you have showed me a whole new world of dreams and possibility. You're my constant inspiration to work hard and achieve more than I ever thought was possible and I couldn't do it without your daily support and smiles. For my dad, Charlie, for supporting me all the way from the other side of the world and treating me to the most delicious meals in London. You're the other half of why food became such an integral part of my life. You make sure my head is in the game at all times – thank you both.

Thank you to Stacey Cleworth, my unbelievably understanding, encouraging and positive editor: there are not enough words in the dictionary to describe your constant sunshine outlook on life. Who would have thought that one DM exchange back in January 2023, when I'd just moved to Japan, would lead to all this? I'm so lucky to be able to work with you and for you to understand my ideas so clearly – you wholeheartedly believed in my vision of wanting to show Japanese home life like I'd imagined. Thank you also to Ellie Spence, for being behind the scenes and making sure everything ran smoothly, always eager and smiley on shoot days!

Thank you to Emily Lapworth, my incredible designer for always being one step ahead and somehow telepathic in making this book. You manage to make the most beautiful and perfect moodboards every time and you've made this book reflect exactly what I wanted it to – calm, serene and beautiful. I couldn't have imagined a book that I'm more proud to call our project!

Thank you to Lizzie Mason for photographing the book in such a bright and beautiful way, working so well with light and texture. And also for bringing the positive energy every morning when anyone walked through the door for the shoot. Thanks also to Lucy Laucht for providing the location shots that so perfectly recall the Japan I describe in the book.

To Esther Clark for creating the stylised mess that I was looking for. You hit the nail on the head, making the book feel so authentic and lived in and, most importantly, accessible. To Emma and Caitlin, for assisting with everything in the kitchen – so much chopping, peeling and frying, but you smashed it out the park. To Anna Wilkins, for the most perfect props – what a treat to have you on board to get so many beautiful little plates, bowls, trinkets and everything in between.

You were the absolute dream team of incredibly inspiring women, I wouldn't have had it any other way!

Thank you so much to Phoebe for continually cheering me on with every new idea and adventure I thought of. Friends for over 20 years and counting, I couldn't have done half of what I've done without you. I'll always be grateful to have you supporting me, always on the other side of the phone when I've had a bright or not-so-bright new idea and also in times of need. You're what makes London feel like home.

Thank you especially to Daniel, for listening to me ramble on about wanting to write a cookbook, and then a zine, then make prints and tea towels and all the other thousand ideas I discussed that day in Kensington Gardens back when we were 21 – so young and full to the brim of ideas, hope and optimism for the future. Who knew that it would hold so much for both of us.

Thank you to Shin, for the support, for always eating my food with a big smile on your face and cooking and cleaning for me when I had to take a break from the kitchen. You've consistently been there for me in a whole new country when I needed it most – I couldn't have begun my journey in Japan so smoothly without you.

To the friends I made on the way. Starting a life in a new country is the most exciting thing you can do, but it's also kind of scary: there's the shock of new culture, new foods to try, new people to meet. I'm so lucky to still have two homes with all the special people who constantly cheer me on and make me smile, laugh and spend hours on end talking to: Sofia, Will and Tegan, Will B, Zoe, Abi, Rina, Masaki, Sylvie, Tanita, Tom, Sofie, Immy, Yumi, Ollie, Alexa, Noah and Nels. It's beyond amazing to have so many people that I so greatly admire and look up to cheering me on my journey, and also have such a thirst and excitement for food and life.

I hope this book inspires you to get out of your comfort zone, whether it's in the kitchen or travelling to a new destination – there's always so much of life to experience and explore.

about the author

Millie Tsukagoshi Lagares is a home cook living in Tokyo. After working in marketing in London's food industry, she left the city and moved to her mother's birthplace, Tokyo, to connect with her heritage and write her first cookbook. Through her recipes, she aims to share the home-cooked soul food of her childhood and demonstrate the accessibility of the cuisine she grew up eating. After starting afresh, the thought of making friends in a new city was certainly an intimidating thought – but one thing that always brings people together is cooking and eating. Throughout the year, this meant plenty of family-style meals, with friends bringing gifts (*omiage*) of freshly caught fish, as well as special ingredients from all over Japan.

Eventually Millie made the move to her own small studio apartment. The shift from cooking for a crowd to navigating a tiny kitchen meant her meals became centred around creating simple dishes using local ingredients in her quintessential pared-back style. Her first book is a collection of effortlessly delicious recipes from her perfect little Japanese kitchen.

Quadrille, Penguin Random House UK, One Embassy Gardens, 8 Viaduct Gardens, London SW11 7BW

Quadrille Publishing Limited is part of the Penguin Random House group of companies whose addresses can be found at global.penguinrandomhouse.com

Copyright
© Millie Tsukagoshi Lagares 2025
Illustrations on page 17
© Millie Tsukagoshi Lagares 2025
Recipe photography
© Lizzie Mayson 2025
Location photography
© Lucy Laucht 2025 on pages 32, 78, 134, 137, 198, 220–21, 227 and 230
Design and Layout
© Quadrille 2025

Millie Tsukagoshi Lagares has asserted her right to be identified as the author of this Work in accordance with the Copyright, Designs and Patents Act 1988

Penguin Random House values and supports copyright. Copyright fuels creativity, encourages diverse voices, promotes freedom of expression and supports a vibrant culture. Thank you for purchasing an authorized edition of this book and for respecting intellectual property laws by not reproducing, scanning or distributing any part of it by any means without permission. You are supporting authors and enabling Penguin Random House to continue to publish books for everyone. No part of this book may be used or reproduced in any manner for the purpose of training artificial intelligence technologies or systems. In accordance with Article 4(3) of the DSM Directive 2019/790, Penguin Random House expressly reserves this work from the text and data mining exception.

Published by Quadrille in 2025

www.penguin.co.uk

A CIP catalogue record for this book is available from the British Library

ISBN 9781837831852
10 9 8 7 6 5 4 3 2 1

Managing Director Sarah Lavelle
Senior Commissioning Editor
Stacey Cleworth
Copy Editor Susan Low
Editorial Assistant Ellie Spence
Art Director & Designer Emily Lapworth
Cover illustrator Emily Lapworth
Internal illustrator
Millie Tsukagoshi Lagares
Photographer Lizzie Mayson
Prop Stylist Anna Wilkins
Food Stylist Esther Clark
Food Stylist Assistants Emma Cantlay and Caitlin Macdonald
Head of Production Stephen Lang
Production Manager Sabeena Atchia

Colour reproduction by F1
Printed in China by C&C Offset Printing Co., Ltd.

The authorised representative in the EEA is Penguin Random House Ireland, Morrison Chambers, 32 Nassau Street, Dublin D02 YH68.

Penguin Random House is committed to a sustainable future for our business, our readers and our planet. This book is made from Forest Stewardship Council® certified paper.